W9-BKF-991

STORIES IN HISTORY

A NATION DIVIDING

1800—1860

nextext

Cover illustration: Todd Leonardo

Printed in the United States of America

ISBN 0-618-14222-3

1 2 3 4 5 6 7 — QKT — 06 05 04 03 02 01

Table of Contents

PART I: TWO WAYS OF LIFE

*Southern planters have trouble producing
enough cotton to make a decent living. Then
Eli Whitney invents the cotton gin. Suddenly,
cotton production is greatly increased, and
now large numbers of slaves are needed. This
side effect worries Northerners.*

*In 1848 gold is found in California. The
population swells so rapidly that California
asks for statehood—as a free state. This
upsets the balance in Congress between free
and slaveholding states. Enter Henry Clay,
with a compromise that helps keep the Union
together for another ten years.*

*John Brown is a violent man. He is against
slavery and is willing to kill those who oppose
his views. Murder in Kansas earns the approval
of some Northerners. When Brown raids
Harpers Ferry in Virginia, however, he goes
too far.*

About this Book

The stories are historical fiction. They are based on historical fact, but some of the characters and events may be fictional. In the Sources section, you'll learn which is which, and where the information came from.

The illustrations are all historical. If they are from a time different from the story, the caption tells you. Original documents help you understand the time period. Maps let you know where things were.

Items explained in People and Terms to Know are repeated in the Glossary. Look there if you come across a name or term you don't know.

Historians do not always know or agree on the exact dates of events in the past. The letter c before a date means "about" (from the Latin word circa*).*

If you would like to read more about these exciting times, you will find recommendations in Reading on Your Own.

Background

"*A house divided against itself cannot stand.*"
I believe this government cannot endure permanently half slave and half free. I do not expect the Union to be dissolved—I do not expect the house to fall—but I do expect it will cease to be divided.

—Abraham Lincoln, 1858

▲

Abraham Lincoln delivers a speech during his 1858 debates with Stephen A. Douglas.

Two Ways of Life

In many ways, America was a divided nation from the start.

In the North

The New England states had rocky soil and a short growing season. Farms were small, and families raised enough to support themselves, with only a

▲
During the first half of the 1800s, factories like this one were built in the North.

little left over to sell. Many people made a living in small businesses—such as building wagons or furniture, making harnesses for horses, and crafting pottery. Shipping, shipbuilding, and fishing were major occupations. By the 1850s in Northern and Middle states, new inventions, such as the sewing machine, and new developments made manufacturing easier. Mills and factories were built. People came from Europe looking for work. In the cities along the Atlantic coast—such as New York, Boston, and Philadelphia—the population grew rapidly.

In the South

Warm temperatures, fertile soil, and a longer growing season led to an economy in the South based on farm products. Tobacco, rice, and later, cotton were grown for sale in Europe as well as at home. Although there were many small farms in the South, there were also huge plantations. The workers on the plantations were slaves.

After Eli Whitney invented the cotton gin in 1793, cotton production became a very big business. Cotton from the South kept the Northern textile, or cloth, mills going. Plantation owners needed more and more workers to harvest their cotton crops. The

▲
The economy of the South in the early 1800s was dominated by the production of a few staple crops, such as the cotton being grown on this Mississippi plantation.

demand for slaves grew, and slavery became very important to the Southern way of life.

In time, two very different lifestyles arose in the two sections. Their different interests caused struggles in the national government. The chief disagreements involved states' rights, tariffs, and slavery.

States' Rights

The issue of states' rights goes back to the beginning of the nation.

The U.S. Constitution—a Contract

When the country was founded, it was made up of independent states. Each had voted to join the nation. The Constitution was a kind of contract that said the states were free in many ways. A great deal of thought and debate had gone into working out the balance of power between state and federal government. Certain parts of the Constitution protected small states from being outvoted by the larger ones. Even back in 1786, there were big differences between the Southern and Northern states.

How Far Do States' Rights Go?

Over the years, many differences were settled, but not always to everyone's liking. A most serious question came up from time to time. Could a state simply reject a federal law that went against its interests? Southern politicians argued that it could. They said such rejection was part of the original contract the states had with each other. Later, they argued that if a state disagreed with the direction Congress or the courts was taking, it had the right to leave the Union. The issue of exactly what were states' rights came up often in the years leading up to the Civil War.

Tariffs

In the early 1800s, British manufacturers were trying to destroy their American competitors. They flooded the American markets with cheap goods. The federal government fought back. It set high taxes, called tariffs, on goods imported from other countries.

In the North. These tariffs helped manufacturing businesses in the North that made the same goods as foreign countries. Tariffs made the imported goods more expensive and Northern goods cheaper for Americans to buy.

In the South. People in the Southern states were used to buying from overseas. They didn't want to buy only Northern goods. They also didn't want to pay more for them.

Even worse, tariffs angered European governments whose manufacturers wanted to sell their things here. Europeans fought back by buying less cotton and fewer farm goods from the South.

The South became angry. People argued at their dinner tables. Editors wrote angry editorials in their newspapers. In Congress, Southern senators and representatives made angry speeches.

Nullification. In 1828, Vice President John C. Calhoun, a Southerner, declared that a state had the right to cancel a federal law that was harmful to it. This canceling was called nullification. Once again, the question of states' rights surfaced—this time over tariffs.

Slavery

What, to the American slave, is your Fourth of July? I answer: A day that reveals to him, more than all other days of the year, the gross injustice and cruelty to which he is the constant victim. To him your celebration is a sham.

—Frederick Douglass, July 4, 1852

Slavery was the most serious issue dividing the North and the South. Slaves had been imported to America since the 1600s, but after January 1, 1808, it was illegal to bring slaves into the country. Even so, the importation of slaves continued illegally. And there was no ban on the slave trade within the United States. Furthermore, the U.S. government made no effort to free those who were already slaves. Although many thought slavery was wrong, people somehow felt that the problem would eventually solve itself. Yet, as the nation grew, so did the slavery question.

Balance Between Slave and Free States

In 1819 there were 22 states—11 free and 11 slave. Although this situation seemed fair enough, the free states had more votes in the House of Representatives because the North had more people than the South. Each Southern state had the same number of senators as each Northern state, but Southerners were worried. They thought the antislavery North might gain too much power. Then Missouri and Maine applied for statehood. Congress reached an agreement in 1820 called the Missouri Compromise. Missouri was admitted as a slave state and Maine as a free one.

Compromise of 1850

Another major question arose when California asked to become a state in 1849. California, whose population had grown greatly after the discovery of gold, wanted to be free, not slave.

By then there were 15 free states and 15 slave states. California's request would upset the balance. Senator Henry Clay proposed several resolutions

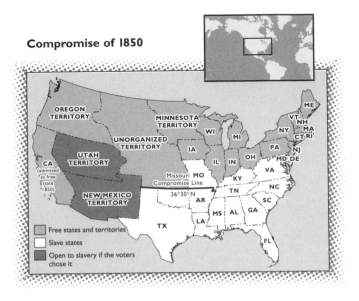

Compromise of 1850

- Free states and territories
- Slave states
- Open to slavery if the voters chose it

that became the Compromise of 1850. One was that California would be admitted as a free state.

Another part of the Compromise dealt with slavery in the District of Columbia. It said that people could own slaves there, but the business of the slave trade would be ended.

Finally, to keep the South happy, the Compromise included the Fugitive Slave Act. This law said that runaway slaves must be returned to their owners. Anyone who helped runaway slaves could be fined $1,000 and put in prison. People who helped capture runaways were paid a reward. There was no protection for any black person seized by slave hunters. Opponents of slavery were outraged.

The Antislavery Movement

I started with this idea in my head, there's two things I've got a right to, death or liberty.

—Harriet Tubman

The first antislavery pamphlet was published by a Quaker in 1762, about a hundred years before the period discussed in this book. But those who wanted to do away with slavery—the abolitionists—were not well organized until the 1800s. As the nation grew, the abolitionist movement gained strength.

Slave Revolts

The Africans who were slaves and their children after them had resisted slavery from the beginning. Sometimes the act was just that of one individual who ran away or who fought back. Sometimes it was a quiet act of resistance, following orders very slowly, for instance. Sometimes it was violent revolt. In 1822, a free black, Denmark Vesey, organized a slave rebellion in Charleston, South Carolina. In 1831, Nat Turner led a slave uprising in Virginia. Neither revolt was successful. Vesey, Turner, and others were killed in the rebellions or executed later.

By the time of Turner's revolt, there were two million slaves. White Southerners were afraid of slave uprisings. The slave states passed laws to limit slaves' movement. There were laws against slaves attending meetings. News of the revolts and of the harsh measures that followed them reached the North. Antislavery feelings grew.

The Underground Railroad

Antislavery societies had existed in the North from the earliest times of the nation. By the 1830s and 1840s, their number and membership had grown. By 1840, an active system was in place for helping runaway slaves reach freedom in the North or in Canada. It is known as the Underground Railroad. Quaker Levi Coffin, escaped slave Harriet Tubman, and many others risked their lives to help slaves to freedom through secret routes and hiding places.

Abolitionists

Many writers and speakers spoke out against slavery. Former slave Frederick Douglass and the Grimké sisters became powerful antislavery leaders. William Lloyd Garrison worked against

▲
An antislavery meeting in Worchester, South Carolina.

slavery in his Massachusetts newspaper, *The Liberator*. Harriet Beecher Stowe's popular book, *Uncle Tom's Cabin*, showed that slaves were human beings, not just property. Many who read it were for the first time aroused to fight slavery.

Kansas–Nebraska Act

In 1854, Congress passed a bill allowing the citizens of Kansas and Nebraska to decide for themselves whether to be free or slave. When proslavery settlers rushed in to Kansas, it became the scene of such violence that it earned the name "Bleeding Kansas."

More Violence

Violence even took place in the Senate. There a Southern representative physically beat a Northern senator for his insulting remarks about a senator from South Carolina.

Dred Scott Decision

Then, in 1857, the Supreme Court ruled that black slave Dred Scott, who had sued to become free, was not a citizen. Therefore, he could not sue to be free, even though he had lived for a time in free states. This ruling meant that no one of African descent was a citizen. Another effect of the decision was to make the Missouri Compromise unconstitutional.

War on the Horizon

John Brown's body lies a-mouldering in the grave,
His soul is marching on!

—Union marching song

In 1859, John Brown, a violent abolitionist, planned a slave rebellion in Virginia. With a small band of whites and blacks, he led an attack on a federal storehouse at Harpers Ferry where weapons were kept. Brown was hanged for treason, but Southern fears of a slave uprising were again fueled.

Many Southerners were tired of the North's attacks on slavery. Southerners felt they needed to defend their way of life. After all, the way Southerners made their living was seriously threatened. Were they to be ruined by these abolitionists? Now, talk of leaving the Union was common. A few Southerners even wanted the African slave trade to become legal again.

When Northerner Abraham Lincoln was elected president in 1860, it was too much for the South. The state of South Carolina was the first to secede, declaring that "the union now subsisting between South Carolina and the other States under the name of the 'United States of America' is hereby dissolved." Although not all Southern citizens were in

Southerners cheer for secession at a meeting in Charleston, South Carolina, in December 1860.

favor of leaving the Union, ten more Southern states seceded. They formed the Confederacy.

When South Carolina troops fired on Fort Sumter, a federal fort in the harbor of Charleston, South Carolina, the Civil War started.

Time Line

1793—Eli Whitney invents the cotton gin.

1820—The Missouri Compromise is passed.

1822—Denmark Vesey's slave revolt fails.

1838—Angelina Grimké's speech in Philadelphia causes a riot.

1848—The California gold rush begins.

1850—P. T. Barnum brings Jenny Lind to New York.

1850—The Compromise of 1850 is passed.

1850—The Fugitive Slave Act becomes law.

1852—*Uncle Tom's Cabin* is published.

1854—The Kansas-Nebraska Act is passed.

1856—Charles Sumner is beaten in the Senate.

1857—The Supreme Court makes the *Dred Scott* decision.

1859—John Brown leads a raid on Harpers Ferry.

1860—Abraham Lincoln is elected president.

1860—South Carolina secedes.

1861—Southern troops fire on Fort Sumter.

Two Ways of Life

The Man and Machine That Changed History

BY JUDITH LLOYD YERO

In 1765, Elias and Elizabeth Whitney of Westboro, Massachusetts, celebrated the birth of their first son, Eli. As he grew, **Eli Whitney** loved to spend time in his father's workshop, fixing things that needed repair. When he was only eight, Eli took apart his father's watch and put it back together again. It ran perfectly.

By the time Eli was twelve, many local men had gone off to fight in the American Revolution. Eli saw a chance to help his family. He set up a **forge** in

---

People and Terms to Know

Eli Whitney—(1765–1825) American inventor best known for his invention of the cotton gin. This invention changed the economy of the South. Whitney also invented the first machines that produced interchangeable parts.

forge—furnace in which metals are heated and shaped.

his father's workshop and began making and selling nails and tools. Later, he added hatpins and metal walking canes.

Eli had many clever ideas to go along with his skillful hands. With his first attempt at business a success, Eli entered Yale College in 1789. At about the same time, George Washington was elected the first president of the newly formed United States of America.

It took ten hours of work to remove the seeds from a single pound of cotton.

After graduation, Eli moved to a Southern **plantation**. The Southern planters had problems producing enough cotton to sell to the cloth makers in the North. Growing and picking cotton were not the problem. The problem was it took ten hours of work to remove the seeds from a single pound of cotton. Preparing cotton for market took too much time to make it a paying crop. Other crops didn't earn enough for plantation owners to keep their slaves, and many were freed. Unfortunately, Whitney changed all of that.

People and Terms to Know

plantation (plan•TAY•shuhn)—large estate or farm on which crops are raised and harvested, often by people who live on the plantation.

As a worker turned the crank on the cotton gin, hooks on the revolving cylinder removed the seeds from the cotton.

A friend of his told the growers that Whitney could help. "He can make anything," she said. Within a few days, Whitney had built a model of a **cotton gin**—a machine that could produce 50 pounds of seed-free cotton a day. A worker turned a handle that cranked the cotton through rollers. Wire teeth on the rollers combed through the cotton, removing the seeds. Another roller with bristles removed the cleaned cotton.

Whitney wrote to his father, "This machine may be turned by water or with a horse, with the greatest ease, and one man and a horse will do more than fifteen men. . . . 'Tis generally said by those who know anything about it, that I shall make a Fortune by it."

People and Terms to Know

cotton gin—machine that removes the seeds from the seed pod of the cotton plant. "Gin" comes from the word *engine*.

The cotton gin was wildly successful. Making a fortune was something else. Whitney got a **patent** for the cotton gin in 1794. He and a partner built many cotton gins around the South. The farmers couldn't buy the machines. They took their cotton to the machines to be cleaned and gave Whitney and his partner part of their cotton in payment. Soon, the planters got tired of paying them. They built copies of the machine. Of course, this was illegal because of Whitney's patent, but that did little good. After ten years of court fights, Whitney received about $90,000. Most of it went to pay his legal bills. Instead of making his fortune, Whitney was penniless. "An invention can be so valuable as to be worthless to the inventor," he said bitterly.

That same year, the cotton crop added nearly ten million dollars to the South's **economy**. Southern planters now needed more workers to grow and pick cotton.

People and Terms to Know

patent (PAT•uhnt)—government grant that gives an inventor the sole right to make, use, and sell an invention for a set period of time.

economy (ih•KAHN•uh•mee)—way in which a country or region makes money; its business affairs.

Eli Whitney simply wanted to invent machines that made people's work easier. Discouraged, he left the South and cotton behind. It was 1797, and a war with France seemed certain. The government needed thousands of guns. Production was very slow because every part of a gun was hand-shaped by skilled workers. Whitney saw a better way.

Whitney's inventions were the beginning of mass production— a process that changed manufacturing forever.

Whitney invented the first milling machines. These machines made gun parts that were interchangeable—that is, they were so much alike that any part would fit any gun. A broken part could be replaced without someone having to work on it to make it fit. Unskilled workers could now quickly make guns as good as those made by highly trained metalworkers. Whitney's inventions were the beginning of mass production—a process that changed manufacturing forever.

By 1850, **King Cotton** reigned in the South. Cotton made up more than 50 percent of the goods

---

People and Terms to Know

King Cotton—term that recognizes that cotton growing was so important to the United States that the laws of the land would support it, just as if it were a king.

the United States shipped to other countries. By 1860 approximately one out of every three Southerners was a slave. White Southerners, especially in the cotton-growing states of South Carolina and Mississippi, were willing to go to war to preserve their way of life.

Forty years after Eli Whitney's death in 1825, the South fell to the superior weapons of the North. Whitney's genius created the victory of King Cotton in the South. It also created the technology with which the North toppled the King.

QUESTIONS TO CONSIDER

1. Why were slaves being freed before the invention of the cotton gin?

2. Why did the cotton gin increase the need for slaves?

3. Why was the cotton gin one of the factors leading to the Civil War?

4. How did Whitney's invention of interchangeable parts help defeat the South in the Civil War?

5. In your opinion, what other inventions have changed the nation's economy?

Eli Whitney: Great Inventor
by Jean Lee Latham

Eli Whitney produced two great inventions, the cotton gin and interchangeable parts that permitted mass production. Together, these two inventions revolutionized the American economy in the first half of the 1800s. Jean Lee Latham's biography tells the story behind Whitney's inventions.

Eli Whitney: Founder of Modern Industry
by Wilma Pitchford Hays

Wilma Pitchford Hays' biography of Eli Whitney presents the story of his career as an inventor and describes his influence on the development of American industry.

Technology's Past:
America's Industrial Revolution and the People Who Delivered the Goods
by Dennis Karwatka

Dennis Karwatka begins his biographical surveys of 76 American scientists, engineers, and inventors with an account of Eli Whitney.

Fanny Kemble: Critic of Slavery

BY STEPHEN CURRIE

Spring 1839

Dearest Anna,

Can it truly have been six months since I last put pen to paper and wrote to you? I am much afraid that it *can*, and indeed *has* been. At present I seem to be spending all my time and energy on this London production of the "**Scottish play**," but too much rehearsal makes me dull, and it is high time I sent you a letter!

People and Terms to Know

Scottish play—William Shakespeare's *Macbeth*, which is set in Scotland. Many actors believe that it is bad luck to say the name of the play.

American artist Thomas Sully painted this portrait of Fanny Kemble in 1833, one year before she married Pierce Butler. The young actress is shown costumed to play Bianca, a character from Shakespeare's play *The Taming of the Shrew*.

At present I am all a-twitter because of a message I have just received from my friend **Fanny Kemble**. You remember Fanny, do you not? You have met her once or twice, I feel certain of it, and of course you know her name. Her Juliet is still much talked about by those who saw it, even though she has now retired from the stage and moved to America. There, you may have heard, she has become known as a critic of slavery, and rightly so, in my opinion. (The notion that one man may own another is terrible. I am glad I am not American!)

But I was speaking of Fanny. She married, you know, and most would say she married well. Her husband, Mr. **Pierce Butler**, is quite wealthy and much admired. He is also—brace yourself, darling—a SLAVEHOLDER!

There! Did I surprise you, dearest Anna? Well, the news surprised me too. It surprised Fanny herself, when she learned the truth after marrying the man. Yes! It is astonishing, but she tells me she had no idea how he had made his money. When he

---

People and Terms to Know

Fanny Kemble—(1809–1893) English actress who first appeared in 1829 as Juliet in Shakespeare's *Romeo and Juliet*. She married an American and spent some time living on his family's plantation. She became known as a strong critic of slavery.

Pierce Butler—(1806–1867) member of an old Southern family, owner of several hundred slaves on a Sea Island plantation, and husband of English actress Fanny Kemble.

mentioned his fine plantation in the **Sea Islands**, she was shocked, but it was too late to back out. (May I ask, however, Anna my dear, that you keep this information private? I know I can count on you.) Men *will* deceive their wives, Anna—it is too bad, too bad. Perhaps 'tis better to be unlucky at love.

So, Fanny writes that the climate in the Sea Islands is delightful, at least in the spring, and that the surroundings are beautiful. Her description reminded me of the stage set when we played together

The island, she says, is beautiful, but that beauty is not real.

in Mr. Shakespeare's **The Tempest**. The theater, however, is not real. The palm trees were only sticks of wood set up for each performance. And the shimmery blue sky was only a backdrop covering the hard brick wall of the back of the stage. So it is with poor Fanny and the island in Georgia. The island, she says, is beautiful, but that beauty is not real.

It is not real, Anna, because the place is cursed with the crime of slavery. This American nation

▲

Slaves on big plantations in the South lived in cabins like those pictured here, at the Hermitage plantation near Savannah, Georgia.

says it believes in liberty and the pursuit of happiness. Yet it allows men to own other human beings as property. Fanny says she considered refusing to go but decided to go with her husband to Georgia after all. It would give her a chance to see slavery in all its misery, she writes.

And misery it is, Anna. The slaves are kept in filth and in ignorance. Fanny writes of their cabins, where two families share a space the size of a sitting room. She tells of their diet: two meals of Indian corn a day. Their clothing is worse. Have you ever played a beggar? I have. The costume was nothing but rags, but it was more than the unfortunate slaves receive—or so Fanny says.

The slaves' ignorance is worse. Slaves know little of the world around them. By law, one may not teach a slave to read or write; one may even be put in jail for doing so. Of course, they do not forbid a man to teach his cow to read, only his slave. I should like to see a man try to teach his cow to read. "What sayest thou, oh mine cow?" he will say, holding up the book, and the cow will say only, "Moo." (A pity Shakespeare did not write such a scene.)

They must labor for six days in the fields, from before dawn till after dusk.

Fanny says, too, that the men and women must perform terribly hard work. Mr. Butler's is a cotton and rice plantation, and his **overseers** give each slave a task to perform each day. So many bags of cotton must be picked, or so many rice plants must be tended. At first Fanny thought the system a good one, for once the task is done, the rest of the day belongs to the slave. But in truth, she writes, the poor slaves are given so much to do that few finish before sunset. They must labor for six days in the fields, from before dawn till after dusk. It is no wonder so many are often ill.

People and Terms to Know

overseers—people who keep watch over and direct the work of others, especially laborers.

Then there are the punishments. Ah, Anna! I wept tears of anger and sorrow when I read Fanny's words. (I am no soft-hearted fool, as you well know; you recall the time I dragged you out of your sickbed so we could perform _Lear_ for the eager crowd in the city of Bath. Say what you will, but the show must go on.) A slave may be beaten for speaking up to the master, for singing at the wrong time, for working too slowly. In short, a slave may be beaten for any reason or for no reason at all. A dozen strokes with the whip is a normal enough punishment. More serious offenses are met with fifty. Think of it, Anna—fifty strokes! Many, Fanny writes, are scarred for life.

Many people in the South believe slavery is good and the slaves are happy! Where is the good when men and women are beaten like animals, I ask? Where is happiness when they are always in fear of the whip? To Mr. Butler, slaves mean money. The plantation, he tells Fanny, turns a fine profit. The work of the slaves helps buy her clothes. At

People and Terms to Know

Lear—Shakespeare's play _King Lear_.

times, Fanny writes, she can scarcely bring herself to wear her beautiful things, knowing that they have been purchased with the blood and sweat of slaves. When she raises the subject of poor treatment, Mr. Butler and his friends talk about the **Irish peasants** and the Northern laborers, and they say that the slave is happier.

Excuse me, Anna, but I must laugh. . . . There! It is an astonishing statement. True, the slave is scarcely worse off in health and home than the paid worker. But the laborer has his liberty. He brings home money, the fruit of his own labors, however tiny the amount. He can leave his work, if he likes. He can move to another town, another country. The slave does not, cannot, may not. The difference is obvious—and yet it means nothing to these men and women of the South.

Ah, Anna, if I dwell on the subject for too long I will go quite mad. Fanny says that perhaps she will turn her thoughts into a book. I hope she will. In the meantime, write me of prettier things. Is anyone

---

People and Terms to Know

Irish peasants—here, poor immigrants from Ireland. Because of English governmental policies, Irish farmers and their families, who did not own the land they farmed, suffered from great poverty in the 1800s. As a result, many moved to the United States.

writing a new drama to suit your talents as a leading lady? Someone should! Are you still considered for the production of *Othello* that was to go on tour next month? I heard that you had a fine chance of playing the **Moor's wife** herself. What a delight that would be. The Moor, by the way, was a black man and *not* a slave, and indeed the hero of the piece! Someone should inform Mr. Butler.

Write when you can, dear friend.

All my love,
Nellie

QUESTIONS TO CONSIDER

1. Why did Fanny Kemble go to the South?

2. How might Kemble have responded to Mr. Butler's claim that the work of the slaves helps buy her clothes?

3. What point is Nellie making when she says, "They do not forbid a man to teach his cow to read, only his slave"?

4. What does the letter tell about the way slavery was viewed by many Southerners of the 1830s?

5. Which of Fanny's observations make the most convincing case against slavery? Why?

People and Terms to Know

Moor's wife—leading role of Desdemona in William Shakespeare's play *Othello*. The Moor is a black North African named Othello, who is married to Desdemona and is the tragic hero of the play.

Fanny Kemble's Journal

During her stay at her husband's plantation, Fanny Kemble was particularly troubled by the situation of the female slaves who were mothers like herself:

"The women who visited me yesterday evening were all in the family way [pregnant], and came to entreat of me to have the sentence (what else can I call it?) modified which condemns them to resume their labor of hoeing in the fields three weeks after their confinement [childbirth]. . . . Their principal spokeswoman . . . appealed to my own experience; and while she spoke of my babies, and my carefully tended, delicately nursed, and tenderly watched confinement and convalescence, and implored me to have a kind of labor given to them less exhausting during the month after their confinement, I held the table before me so hard in order not to cry out that I think my fingers ought to have left a mark on it."

Daily Life on a Southern Plantation, 1853
by Paul Erickson

Paul Erickson describes the very different ways of life of a white family and black family who both live at Waverly, a cotton plantation in New Iberia, Louisiana. The white family is the Hendersons, who own Waverly. The black family is that of Daddy Major, chief driver on the plantation.

Sisters Against Slavery: A Story About Sarah and Angelina Grimké
by Stephanie Sammartino McPherson

Stephanie Sammartino McPherson tells the story of two sisters from a wealthy Southern family who, like Fanny Kemble, spoke out against slavery.

Fanny Kemble's America
by John Anthony Scott

John Anthony Scott's biography presents the life and times of the famous English actress who recorded her observations of slavery on her husband's plantation.

Frederick Douglass's Escape to Freedom

BY LYNNETTE BRENT

A man sat on the train bound for New York City. His eyes were closed, but the soft sounds of a song were coming from his mouth.

> *I'll fly away, O glory, I'll fly away.*
> *When I die, hallelujah, by and by,*
> *I'll fly away.*

<u>Frederick Douglass</u> thought back to another long, difficult journey. He was small, barely six years old at the time. He remembered clinging to

People and Terms to Know

Frederick Douglass—(c. 1817–1895) runaway slave who became a famous Northern abolitionist, publisher, and public speaker. He advised Lincoln on slavery and later became U.S. Minister to Haiti.

THE FUGITIVE'S SONG,

WORDS

composed and respectfully dedicated, in token of confident esteem to

FREDERICK DOUGLASS

A Graduate from the

"PECULIAR INSTITUTION"

LITH. of E.W. BOUVÉ

This cover for the sheet music for "The Fugitive's Song" is illustrated with an imaginary picture of Frederick Douglass's escape from slavery. Written in 1845, the song was dedicated to him "for his courage, ability, and achievements in the antislavery cause."

the hem of his grandmother's dress as they traveled from his home to the Lloyd plantation. The home was large and fancy. Grandmother hugged Frederick hard, then pointed out three other children in the yard. "Those are your brother and sisters. Go on and join them." Frederick did as she asked and helped the children with their chores. As night fell, Frederick began to worry. He hadn't seen his grandmother in hours. Where was she? It was time to go home. His brother told him that his grandmother had left. Frederick fell to the ground, crying.

At the Lloyd Plantation, Frederick learned about the harsh realities of slavery.

That was the first understanding that Frederick had of slavery. At the Lloyd Plantation, Frederick learned about the harsh realities of slavery. He was used to living with his grandmother. He had food and clothing and played in the woods all day. At the plantation, the children were fed cornmeal mush out of a tray for animals' food. They were given one shirt each. Instead of using beds, the children slept on the kitchen floor. Frederick also saw his first beating.

Some glad morning when life is over,
I'll fly away.
To a home on God's celestial shore,
I'll fly away.

Frederick's train continued on from Pennsylvania to New York. He remembered yet another trip. When he was eight years old, he was sent to Baltimore, Maryland, to live with his master's relatives. The Baltimore gentleman, Hugh Auld, was a shipbuilder. Frederick ran errands and helped care for the Aulds' infant son. Frederick also got his first pair of new pants since leaving his grandmother's cabin.

Hugh Auld's wife was very religious. Frederick loved to listen to her sing hymns and read from her Bible. One day, Mrs. Auld invited Frederick to sit with her as she read. She showed him the letters on the page. She taught him the sounds that the letters made. Soon, Frederick was reading.

Mrs. Auld was very proud of how quickly Frederick learned. She showed her husband what Frederick could do. Instead of being pleased, Hugh Auld was furious. Teaching a slave to read was against the law. If slaves could learn to read, their owners feared that they would think too much and fight back. If slaves could learn to write, they could make false papers that could set them free. Mr. Auld ordered that the lessons stop immediately.

> *When the shadows of this life have gone,*
> *I'll fly away.*
> *Like a bird from prison bars has flown,*
> *I'll fly away.*

Hugh Auld's reaction to Frederick's learning taught Frederick an important lesson. It taught Frederick that he could escape slavery by continuing to learn to read and write. While he was running errands for the Aulds, he met poor white children. He gave them bread in exchange for reading lessons. Mrs. Auld caught him reading many times, but Frederick continued to disobey. He bought a book of speeches on freedom and began reading about **abolition** in the newspaper. This was the first that Frederick had heard of people wanting to end slavery. Frederick was twelve years old then, and these new ideas meant everything to him. Frederick began to teach other young slaves to read, knowing that this would be the way to freedom.

People and Terms to Know

abolition (AB•uh•LIHSH•uhn)—act of ending slavery. A person who wants to end slavery is called an abolitionist.

Just a few more weary days and then,
I'll fly away.
To a land where joys shall never end,
I'll fly away.

Frederick was sent to Thomas Auld, a relative of Hugh Auld. Thomas Auld treated his slaves terribly. He starved them and beat them often. When Thomas Auld discovered that Frederick was organizing religious services for other slaves, he felt that Frederick was too unruly, and sent him away to Edward Covey, a "slave breaker."

Frederick soon understood what "slave breaker" meant.

Frederick was glad for the change at first. At least there was more food. However, Frederick soon understood what "slave breaker" meant. For months, Frederick was whipped daily for offenses as simple as resting or not controlling the animals properly in the field. Some days, he was beaten so badly that he collapsed from the pain. He begged the Auld family to take him back, but they refused.

After six months, Frederick could take it no more. He grabbed Covey by the throat and fought back. The two struggled and fought for two hours. Finally, Covey gave up. Covey could have had Frederick killed for fighting, but he did nothing. Covey didn't want it known that he was beaten by a 16-year-old boy.

Frederick worked for Covey for a year, then for another master until he was 18. They didn't beat or whip him after he had stood up to Edward Covey. Frederick continued to teach other slaves how to read and write. They met at night and on Sundays. He also began planning to escape.

> *I'll fly away, O glory, I'll fly away.*
> *When I die, hallelujah, by and by,*
> *I'll fly away.*

That was two years ago. Since then, Frederick had worked again for Hugh Auld in Baltimore. In those two years, he met with educated former slaves, who taught Frederick even more. He hoped to escape, but it would require money. During his time off, Frederick was able to work for a local shipbuilder. Hugh Auld took most of the money that Frederick earned, so it took a long time to save what was needed.

This was also the time that Frederick met Anna Murray. She was a free black woman who worked as a servant for another local family. Frederick and Anna fell in love and became engaged. As much as he hated slavery, he was living a comfortable life. How could he run away and leave Anna behind? Trying to escape was dangerous. If Frederick were caught, he could be sold to slave traders or killed. Yet, after an argument with Hugh Auld, Frederick decided that escaping was his only choice.

Then, two days ago, with Anna's money, Frederick bought a train ticket to Philadelphia. He borrowed a free friend's identification papers and sailor's clothing as a **disguise**. The next day, he boarded the train. The conductor in the "Negro car" asked to see his papers as the train reached the Pennsylvania border. Frederick was terribly nervous. He didn't match the description on the identification papers. The conductor looked at the papers quickly and walked away. Frederick was on his way to freedom.

As Frederick saw the lights of New York City through the window, he was grateful for his decision. It was September 8, 1838. He was a free man.

People and Terms to Know

disguise—use of changed dress or appearance to hide one's true identity.

* * *

Frederick Douglass married Anna Murray after arriving in New York City in 1838. He became famous worldwide for speaking for the right of liberty. Not only was he an abolitionist, he also was a supporter of women's rights. He wrote in newspapers that taught thousands about the antislavery movement, and he helped many escape slavery through the Underground Railroad. He was an advisor to President Lincoln during the Civil War. He also acted as an advisor to the government after the war, helping freed slaves adjust to their new lives. Later, he was a U.S. marshal for the District of Columbia and American representative to the Republic of Haiti.

QUESTIONS TO CONSIDER

1. How would you describe Frederick Douglass?
2. Why do you think there were differences in the ways that some slaveholders treated their slaves?
3. Why wouldn't the slave owners want their slaves to know how to read?
4. What was the function of a "slave breaker"?

Narrative of the Life of Frederick Douglass

After escaping from slavery and becoming involved in the antislavery movement, Frederick Douglass wrote in his autobiography:

"If at any one time of my life more than another I was made to drink the bitterest dregs of slavery, that time was during the first six months of my stay with this man Covey. We worked all weathers. It was never too hot or too cold. It could never rain, blow, snow, or hail too hard for us to work in the field. Work, work, work was as much the order of the night as the order of the day. I had neither time to eat or sleep. I was somewhat unmanageable at first, but a few months of Covey's discipline tamed me. He succeeded in breaking me in body, soul, and spirit. My natural elasticity was crushed, my intellect languished, the wish to read departed, and the dark night of slavery closed in upon me."

Young Frederick Douglass: The Slave Who Learned to Read
by Linda Walvoord Girard

Frederick Douglass was born a slave. He fought back to become the greatest African-American leader of the 1800s. Linda Walvoord Girard's account focuses on the young Douglass's desire to read and the effect that learning to read had on his later career in the antislavery movement.

Escape to Freedom: A Play About Young Frederick Douglass
by Ossie Davis

The well-known African-American playwright Ossie Davis uses narrative, dialogue, and song to tell the inspiring story of how the young Douglass began his fight against slavery.

Escape from Slavery: The Boyhood of Frederick Douglass in His Own Words
edited by Michael McCurdy
(foreword by Coretta Scott King)

Michael McCurdy presents a shortened version of Douglass's own account of his early life.

P. T. Barnum and New York City

BY MARIANNE McCOMB

There were close to thirty thousand people watching as the young woman stepped off the steamship docked in New York Harbor. **P. T. Barnum**, who had seen plenty in his life, had never seen anything quite like this. Thousands stood cheering on the docks. Even more stood on the sidewalks above the harbor. Barnum looked around. *All this for one woman!* he marveled. And it was he, P. T. Barnum, who had arranged the whole thing! To Barnum, that was the most marvelous part of all.

People and Terms to Know

P. T. Barnum—(1810–1891) Phineas Taylor Barnum, multimillionaire American showman, who specialized in unusual, inexpensive entertainment.

This cartoon, "Panorama of Humbug," pokes fun at P. T. Barnum's publicity campaign to promote the concert tour of Swedish singer Jenny Lind. A huge poster of Lind is back of the stage. Musicians in the orchestra below blow trumpets labeled with the names of various newspapers. Barnum himself stands in the doorway of the ticket office.

The woman who walked off the ship that day in 1850 was **Jenny Lind**, an opera singer from Sweden who was said to have the voice of an angel. The man who waited to greet her, P. T. Barnum, was as famous in his own country as she was in hers. Barnum had been waiting six months for the "Swedish Nightingale" to arrive in New York. He had arranged for her visit, paid for her trip, and booked concerts for her all over New York. His plan, he said, was to introduce New Yorkers to the finer things in life.

To many, Barnum was the King of Hoaxes, the Prince of Humbugs.

Some people were surprised by Barnum's plan. To many, Barnum was the King of Hoaxes, the **Prince of Humbugs**. Barnum himself loved these titles. He had worked hard to earn them.

Phineas Taylor Barnum was born on July 5, 1810, in Bethel, Connecticut. When Barnum was 15 years old, his father died, and young Phineas

---

People and Terms to Know

Jenny Lind—(1820–1887) talented singer born in Stockholm, Sweden. She toured the United States from 1850 to 1852.

Prince of Humbugs—nickname for P. T. Barnum. A humbug is something meant to fool people; a fake or a hoax. Barnum loved to play pranks on people. Many of his exhibits turned out to be hoaxes, or fakes, but the crowds still loved his shows.

had to support the family. He worked a number of different jobs and finally ended up selling lottery tickets.

When he was 19 years old, Barnum married Charity Hallet, a local girl with a pretty laugh. Five years later, in 1834, lotteries were banned in the state of Connecticut. Instead of being discouraged, Barnum announced that he would move. He wouldn't move South. The South was filled with farms and plantations, and the population was relatively small. What he needed, he knew, was a big city with lots of people. In the North, there were a couple of large cities to choose from. He decided that it made the most sense to choose the largest of them all—New York City. He would take his wife and new baby to New York City and make his fortune there.

If Barnum expected New York to greet him with open arms, he was sadly mistaken. At the time, New York City had a population of around two hundred fifty thousand. Almost everyone there was also looking to make a fortune. There were hundreds of businesses in the city. Most were owned by wealthy men who had lived in New York for years and years. The only opportunity for a man like Barnum was to work long hours for little pay.

Eventually, Barnum took a job selling hats and ties. He made only a few dollars a week, but he saved as much as he could.

In the spring of 1835, Barnum met a man who had seen a very strange exhibit. The exhibit featured the supposed 161-year-old nurse of George Washington. Out of curiosity, Barnum arranged to meet this "nurse," whose name was Joice Heth.

The moment he met Heth, Barnum knew he was looking at a gold mine. The ancient, shriveled woman certainly *looked* old enough to be 161. Without hesitating, Barnum arranged a deal and brought Heth back to New York. He hung posters all over the city. He submitted articles to the newspapers telling about this "astonishing" woman.

Barnum's Heth exhibit was typical of the kind of "shows" that New Yorkers of the time loved to see. On weekends, whole families went from one theater to another to watch live performances of acrobats, jugglers, dancers, and the like. They also went to shows that featured men, women, and children who had an interesting story to tell. Barnum knew that New Yorkers would want to hear Heth's story.

People came from all over the city to see Heth. Barnum began selling $1,500 worth of tickets a week.

At last, Barnum had found a business. He would be a showman, he decided, and make a million dollars.

In 1837, however, Barnum and the rest of New York were swept into a terrible **financial depression**. All over the city, business owners went bankrupt. Over the next three years, hundreds of the stores, newspapers, and businesses that had long been an important part of New York life closed their doors.

These three hundred thousand New Yorkers had to be entertained somehow, didn't they?

By 1841, the economy in New York City had partially recovered. There were now close to four hundred thousand men, women, and children living in New York. It was by far the largest city in America. Barnum saw opportunity in these numbers. After all, he reasoned, these three hundred thousand New Yorkers had to be entertained somehow, didn't they?

Barnum walked the city in search of a place to hold his shows of the strange and fantastic. Finally, he found a place on Broadway, the busiest street in

---

People and Terms to Know

financial depression—serious reduction in business activity. During a depression, many people lose their jobs.

the city. Day and night, Broadway was a river of thousands of carriages, horses, wagons, and people. At one of the busiest intersections on Broadway stood a five-story building once known as the American Museum. The owner of the museum had lost all his money during the depression and was forced to sell. Barnum took over the five-story building and renamed it Barnum's American Museum.

Barnum's museum was an instant hit. New Yorkers, who had just lived through three long years of a depression, were desperate to have some fun. They came in big crowds to see Barnum's unusual exhibits. Some of his most popular ones included the Feejee Mermaid (a woman who had the body of a fish), Chang and Eng (twins who were joined at the chest), and Vantile Mack (a seven-year-old boy who weighed 257 pounds).

One of Barnum's most successful exhibits ever was the show he created for General Tom Thumb. Tom Thumb, who was born Charles Sherwood Stratton, was just 25 inches tall when Barnum first saw him. Barnum spent months teaching Tom to sing, dance, and act. Then he began advertising the "most surprising and delightful curiosity the world

Barnum is shown with one of his most famous exhibits, Tom Thumb.

has ever known." Audiences were thrilled with the tiny General and came back to the museum again and again to see Tom perform.

Thanks to the successes of his shows, Barnum became a millionaire many times over. Still he hungered for more. The people of New York, he said, needed some culture. There was more to entertainment than shows featuring fat children and bearded ladies. So Barnum began scouting for a "class" act, one that would introduce the arts to this huge city.

At the time, only rich New Yorkers attended operas, ballets, and quality theater. The tickets for this type of entertainment were too expensive for most New Yorkers. Barnum's idea was to stage a quality act at an affordable price. Jenny Lind, he knew, would fit the bill.

Barnum had never heard Lind sing, but he knew that she was hugely popular overseas. Her high, pure voice had been thrilling European audiences for years. Famous composers wrote music especially for her. The storyteller Hans Christian Andersen wrote his story "The Nightingale" in honor of her.

In early 1850, Barnum offered to pay for Lind to come to America. After carefully considering Barnum's offer, Lind agreed and said she would arrive in September.

Barnum had six months to convince his fellow New Yorkers that a Jenny Lind concert was worth seeing. He gave newspaper reporters information about her music. He plastered posters all over the city and hung huge pictures of Lind outside his museum. He encouraged doll makers to make a Jenny Lind doll and hat makers to make a Jenny Lind hat. Soon there were Jenny Lind shawls,

Jenny Lind stoves, Jenny Lind carriages, and Jenny Lind cigars. The people of New York began competing with each other to see how many Jenny Lind products they could buy.

When Barnum began selling tickets to Lind's concerts, all of New York went crazy. People stood in line for hours, their pockets stuffed with coins. The response was so great that Barnum scheduled ten more New York shows for Lind— even though she had not yet sung in America.

Her high, clear voice soared, and the audience grew silent in wonder.

Lind arrived in New York on September 1, 1850. Thirty thousand people jammed the harbor and lined the streets to greet her. When she stepped off the steamship, the crowd went wild.

Lind's first concert was held at Castle Garden, which was located on an island in New York harbor. Five thousand lucky New Yorkers came to hear her sing. Some people were disappointed when they first saw Lind. She was actually quite plain. But when she began to sing, people forgot their disappointment. Her high, clear voice soared, and the audience grew silent in wonder. Lind sang for over an hour that night. The beauty of her voice made many New Yorkers cry.

When Lind came out to take her bows, the audience cheered until Barnum himself came out on stage too. The two of them—Jenny Lind and P. T. Barnum—stood side by side onstage and smiled as five thousand New Yorkers jumped to their feet and applauded. It was one of Barnum's finest moments.

* * *

In all, close to 82 million people visited Barnum's American Museum before it burned to the ground in 1868. Shortly after that, Barnum began scouting around for something else to do. In 1881, he formed a partnership with a man named James A. Bailey. Together, they created the Barnum and Bailey Circus, and they billed it as "the greatest show on earth." Barnum's circus, like almost everything else he was involved in, became a great success.

QUESTIONS TO CONSIDER

1. What challenges did Barnum face when he moved to New York?

2. How did the financial depression of the late 1830s change Barnum's fortunes?

3. Why do you think New Yorkers went to Barnum's American Museum?

4. What does this story tell you about life in the North before the Civil War?

Put Up Your Dukes!

BY WALTER HAZEN

Each evening I sit on the porch and rock the time away. My dog Sandy always joins me. I think she could rock, too, if she put her mind to it. She's mighty smart.

I sit here and think about the great war that is coming. I could be a part of it if it weren't for my sister Rose. What a snitch! The day I sneaked off to sign up as a drummer boy, she told Papa. Boy! My ear hurt for a long time after he dragged me out of that recruiting place and took me home.

"You're only 14!" he scolded. "You're too young to join up and fight. Now get yourself home before I tan the daylights out of you!"

In this cartoon, figures representing England and France encourage the South and North to fight. The snake represents Northerners—called Copperheads—that sympathized with the South.

So here I sit and think about what caused this war. Papa puts the blame directly on the Rebs and slavery. He says that if the South had freed its slaves as the North had done, the war would never have started.

Then there's the **tariffs**. They're some kind of tax on goods brought into the country. The North and the South constantly argued about 'em.

My teacher said that, around 1832, South Carolina got so mad over a tariff that it threatened to quit the Union. Yeah—just flat quit! I think they call that **secession**. People in South Carolina and the other Southern states were against the tariff because it made the price of fancy clothes and fancy furniture from England really high. The Northern clothing and furniture manufacturers, however, liked the tariff because they could sell their stuff at a cheaper price.

People and Terms to Know

tariffs (TAIR•ihfs)—taxes on goods coming into or going out of a country. See pages 15–16.

secession (sih•SEHSH•uhn)—act of withdrawing from the Union (the United States). .

Anyhow, South Carolina backed off, and things calmed down for a while. Then other problems popped up. The North and the South argued about slavery spreading westward. Papa explained it to me this way: the North was "agin" it, while the South was for it. Southerners wanted to take slaves into the western territories, and Northerners wanted to keep them out. Both sides "put up their dukes," and feelings ran pretty high.

Both sides "put up their dukes," and feelings ran pretty high.

Several times, when tempers really flared and it seemed that war was sure to break out, a **compromise** was reached. The way I hear it, a man named **Henry Clay** came up with an idea that put off war for a while.

Never mind that the North and the South became like two different worlds. Folks from each part of the country said such outrageous things about the other, it made me laugh.

People and Terms to Know

compromise (KAHM•pruh•MYZ)—agreement in which each side in a dispute gives up some of its demands.

Henry Clay—(1777–1852) statesman who served as a U.S. senator and a congressman from Kentucky. Clay put together the Compromise of 1850, which kept the Union together for 10 more years. (See pages 17–18.)

▲
Published just before the Civil War, this cartoon shows Southerners cutting themselves off from the Union.

A Georgia newspaper editor said the North was "a hodge-podge of greasy mechanics, filthy laborers, small-fisted farmers, and moon-struck idealists!" He said that while Southerners were a "master race," Northerners were faceless and the enemies of "gentility." Gentility has something to do with being a gentleman, I'm sure.

Mama and Papa talked about how Southern slave owners were always saying that slavery was a necessary part of their lives. Without slavery, they said, their world would crumble.

"But how," I asked one time, "can people in the South not feel bad about having slaves?"

"Well," Papa answered, "they say their slaves are better off than our mill workers here in the North. They seem to believe that all our mill workers live in slums and are dirt poor. They say that slaves all have a home and a guaranteed job. They have people to take care of them when they are sick or become old. Maybe it's so, maybe it's not."

Well, so much for Southerners and their opinion of us. Here in the North, I can remember abolitionists calling slave owners "awful monsters." They believed that every slave was one big gob of welts and burns—or worse. They also said that Southerners were sneaky and always out for revenge. I remember the preacher once saying that Southerners were "vainglorious braggarts." I looked up *vainglorious*. It means something like arrogant or boastful.

Well, I'm not vainglorious, but I sure am an enemy of gentility. I sure wish I could do something about it! I hear they're training boys to be sharpshooters up in Vermont. Could I get there somehow? Sandy, ol' girl, what do you think?

QUESTIONS TO CONSIDER

1. Why did South Carolina threaten to secede from the Union in 1832?

2. How did the South justify slavery?

3. What effect do you think the name-calling had on the disputes between the North and South?

4. Why do you think the narrator wants to train for the war that is coming?

5. What does the narrator's account tell you about America in the years before the Civil War?

The Question
of Slavery

The Rebellion That Never Was

BY STEPHEN FEINSTEIN

The old slave known simply as Jack sat beneath the magnolia tree with twelve other slaves belonging to Master Loomis. Before them stood a black man who looked to be in his fifties. He was well dressed, and he called himself **Denmark Vesey**. The name sounded strange to Jack.

Vesey told the group he had walked all the way from Charleston, South Carolina, which was about ten miles away. He said that he had come to bring them a very important message. In time, he and his friends would deliver this message to all the plantation slaves in the neighborhood of Charleston.

People and Terms to Know

Denmark Vesey (VEE•zee)—(c. 1767–1822), free black carpenter who planned and organized a slave rebellion in South Carolina.

The most famous and violent slave revolt was the one led by Nat Turner in Southampton County, Virginia, in 1831. Here, Turner is being captured.

Vesey then began to talk to the group gathered before him. He spoke forcefully, and he spoke of God. To Jack, Vesey sounded like a preacher. In fact, he carried a Bible with him. From time to time he read passages from it. He said that, although he had been born a slave just like them, he had become a free man. The time was coming, he said, when all black people would be free. When Vesey spoke of freedom, a fire seemed to burn within him. People were not meant to live in slavery, he said. It was terribly wrong. Vesey opened his Bible again and read, "And he that stealeth a man, and selleth him . . . shall surely be put to death."

The slaves were quiet at these words. Jack looked at the others. There were looks of fear on their faces. These were dangerous words indeed. But Vesey went on. He said that the time was near at hand when African slaves and those of African descent would rise up and kill the masters. Then they would be truly free. Vesey read from his Bible, "And they utterly destroyed all that were in the city, both man and woman, both young and old."

The slaves sat in shock, barely able to breathe. Jack looked over his shoulder to make sure Barton the slaves' overseer was nowhere near. Vesey then described the **revolt** that he and his friends were planning. Once they had organized a large enough force of slaves, they would attack the city of Charleston. There they would raid the city's **arsenal** and seize guns. The city would be burned to the ground. All of the white people except for a few sea captains would be killed. The sea captains would be forced to help the rebels escape by sea. The slaves, now free men and women, would sail away to Africa, or perhaps to Haiti. Vesey told the slaves that they would be very welcome in Haiti. He told them about **Toussaint L'Ouverture**, the former black slave who had led a successful slave revolt against Haiti's white rulers. Haiti was now a black nation.

The city would be burned to the ground.

People and Terms to Know

revolt—armed uprising; rebellion against a government.

arsenal (AHR•suh•nuhl)—place for storing or repairing weapons and ammunition.

Toussaint L'Ouverture (too•SAN loo•vehr•TYOOR)—(c. 1743–1803) Haitian slave and freedom fighter who helped Haiti win independence.

Jack wasn't so sure he liked Vesey's message. The idea of freedom was wonderful. Jack had heard many times the story of how Moses led the Jews out of slavery in Egypt. He noticed how Vesey's eyes lit up whenever he referred to that story. But killing all those people—men, women, and children—that didn't sound right. Jack looked up at Vesey and dared to challenge him. "All that killing—it's not right . . . it's not right!" he said, shaking his head.

Vesey looked sternly at Jack and simply said, "The Lord has commanded it." He then said good-bye to the slaves of the Loomis Plantation. Vesey had many miles to go before dark. He promised Jack and the other slaves that they would be hearing from him from time to time as plans for the revolt took shape. He would look forward to greeting them when the time of their freedom was at hand. Vesey then walked off down the road to the next plantation along the river.

* * *

It was now June 1822. Four years had passed since Vesey had first visited the Loomis Plantation. The plans for the slave revolt had finally come together. At midnight on Sunday, June 16, Denmark

Vesey and about nine thousand black slaves would rise up against the white people of Charleston. By early Sunday evening, hundreds of slaves from the surrounding plantations were streaming down the roads toward Charleston.

Jack and six of the other slaves had slipped away from the Loomis Plantation shortly after sunset. As he walked along in the dark, Jack felt as though he and his companions were heading toward disaster.

He and the others had been thinking about nothing but freedom for the past four years.

Often he had been doubtful about the planned revolt. Yet he and the others had been thinking about nothing but freedom for the past four years. Now Jack wanted freedom so badly he could almost taste it. No price was too high to pay for it.

It was almost midnight. Charleston was less than a mile away. Jack and the others rounded a bend in the road—and stopped short. Up ahead, a fire was flickering by the roadside. They could see a group of men in the road. The road was blocked with trees that had been chopped down. The men all had guns. They were soldiers! "Who goes there?" a voice cried out.

Although the night air was cool, Jack broke out in a sweat. In a flash, he and the others knew what had happened. Somehow, the whites must have found out about Vesey's plot. Jack remembered the strange black man who had come by the plantation that week. He had seemed very interested in their talk about the revolt. And he had asked a lot of questions. Why had they trusted him? He must have talked to the white authorities. And if not him, some other person like him.

Jack and his companions fled back down the road. They arrived back at the plantation before sunrise. Their dream of freedom had been crushed. Later they would learn that they were among the lucky ones. About 130 blacks were arrested. There were trials shortly afterward. Denmark Vesey and 34 of the leaders of the plot were hanged.

For a time, life for the slaves at the Loomis Plantation was almost unbearable. They had been so close to freedom only to have their hopes ended. Jack was an old man. He had been a slave all his life, and he knew he would die a slave. Someday, though, Jack believed, freedom would come for the black people. Freedom was too powerful an idea to be forever denied.

QUESTIONS TO CONSIDER

1. What were Vesey's plans for making his revolt a success?

2. Why did Jack object to Vesey's plan at first?

3. How did Vesey justify the killing of whites?

4. According to Jack, how was Vesey's plan uncovered?

5. If you had been a slave living in or near Charleston in 1822, what would you have done if Vesey had asked you to join the revolt, and why?

Angelina Grimké Starts a Riot

BY CAROLE POPE

My hero was **Angelina Grimké**. You might think it strange, me a young, free black woman and all, and Angelina a young, white abolitionist barely into her thirties. But believe me, Angelina Grimké changed my life for all time.

It was May 1838. Freedom-loving men and women, both black and white, were beginning to speak out against slavery. Because the abolitionists were not allowed to speak in many public buildings in Philadelphia, they built their own meeting hall. This building, which held three thousand people, was one of the most beautiful in the city. People of many different religious beliefs helped to build the meeting hall. It

---

People and Terms to Know

Angelina Grimké (GRIHM•kee)—(1805–1879) American antislavery and women's rights leader; sister of Sarah Grimké (1792–1873).

Portrait of Angelina Grimké in Quaker dress.

was dedicated to the free expression of ideas, liberty, and civil rights. Pennsylvania Hall, the "temple of freedom" as it was called, opened on May 14, 1838.

Angelina became my friend the day she and her sister, Sarah Grimké, walked into the **Quaker** meetinghouse and sat down on the "colored bench," the place reserved for black people. As Angelina squeezed into the seat next to me, I nearly died of surprise. We weren't used to white women doing such things. The Grimké sisters didn't like the thought of us sitting separately in a place of worship, so they joined us.

She secretly taught her personal maidservant, a slave, to read.

Angelina and Sarah were the daughters of a wealthy, slave-owning family from Charleston, South Carolina. Angelina told me how Sarah had influenced her thoughts about slavery. Sarah, the older sister, had seen the beating of a slave as a young child. Later, when she was much older, she secretly taught her personal maidservant, a slave, to read. They met each night and read together by firelight. When Sarah's father found out, he was angry and threatened to

People and Terms to Know

Quaker—Christian group that opposes war and violence; also called the Society of Friends.

have Sarah's maidservant beaten. Sarah knew that was wrong. Strongly opposed to slavery, she left home, moved to Philadelphia, and became a Quaker.

Angelina was curious about her older sister's views. She explained that she had been different from Sarah. She liked lace and fancy clothes and spent a lot of time reading romance novels. After learning more about her sister's new Quaker beliefs, Angelina made a decision. "Today I have torn up my novels," she wrote in her diary. She also went through her fancy clothes and threw them on the bed. Angelina told me that she no longer felt comfortable in her pretty clothes.

Angelina said that the next summer, when she was twenty-two, she visited Sarah in Philadelphia. There, she found herself surrounded by Quakers. Because she was from the South, she was often urged to give her opinions about slavery. She had never openly spoken out against slavery as her older sister had. That summer she changed.

She went home dressed in the plain clothes that Quakers wore. She tried to convince her friends and family to give up slavery. Few of them agreed with her. Angelina's friends—and even her brother—criticized and deserted her. Finally she realized that Charleston was no longer her home. In 1829 she went back to Philadelphia to begin a new life with her sister. She left the Presbyterian Church and became a Quaker. In Philadelphia she lived a different life from before. She did chores that slaves had done and shopped for food at open-air markets.

Angelina also began to speak on abolition in public. On May 16, 1838, only two days after her marriage to abolitionist Theodore Weld, she spoke to an antislavery convention of American women at Pennsylvania Hall. The new building had opened just two days earlier. Angelina gave her speech to a packed audience of both blacks and whites at the hall. I'll never forget when she said:

> "We often hear the question asked, 'What shall we do?' Here is an opportunity for doing something now. Every man and every woman present may do something by showing that we fear not a mob, and, in the midst of threatenings and revilings [name-calling], by opening our mouths for the dumb and pleading the cause of those who are ready to perish."

She also said that women could do little to help slaves until they were free themselves. Many of us present were thrilled by her words. But there was an angry mob of men both inside and outside the hall. They grew increasingly loud and threatening. They tried to interrupt her speech with hateful shouts, but she merely spoke above them. Those outside

I was frightened, but Angelina's quiet courage helped steady me.

threw rocks at the windows. We heard the sound of breaking glass. I was frightened, but Angelina's quiet courage helped steady me. After her speech, we went home, but the mob remained.

Early the next morning we returned to finish the business of the convention. The mayor had a different idea. He was afraid there would be more rioting. He suggested postponing the meetings and had the hall cleared. The mob cheered the mayor, sent him on his way, and then promptly stormed the hall. I stood in the street, horrified at what happened next. The men broke windows, piled up all the books inside, and set fire to them. Soon the beautiful new hall was in flames. The police and fire departments did not try to put out the fire. At the end, only the outer walls of the building remained.

I often think back to that night. I can still hear Angelina's voice inside my head. She gave me the courage to speak out against slavery. We won against slavery in the end, but we had to fight a war. Now I speak out for the right of women to vote. Most of all, I thank Angelina for giving me the firm belief in my place and importance in the world.

*   *   *

Angelina and Theodore Weld, along with Sarah, moved away from Philadelphia shortly after the fire. Because of an injury, Angelina Grimké never spoke in public again. Until their deaths, the sisters continued to fight against slavery and for the right of women to vote. They paved the way for such **suffragists** as **Susan B. Anthony** and **Elizabeth Cady Stanton**.

People and Terms to Know

suffragists (SUHF•ruh•jists)—people who fight for the extension of voting rights, especially for women.

Susan B. Anthony—(1820–1906) one of the first campaigners for women's rights, including the right to vote.

Elizabeth Cady Stanton—(1815–1902) leader who worked throughout her life, much of the time in partnership with Susan B. Anthony, to help gain rights for women.

QUESTIONS TO CONSIDER

1. What events in each of their lives caused Angelina and Sarah to take up the abolitionist cause?

2. Why do you think some men were angered and threatened by Angelina's speeches?

3. How do you think the destruction of Pennsylvania Hall could have been stopped?

4. Why was Angelina Grimké such an important model for the young woman who tells this story?

Primary Source

What Is a Mob?

During her speech at Pennsylvania Hall, Angelina Grimké commented on the disturbance:

"What is a mob? What would the breaking of every window be? What would the leveling of this Hall be? . . . What if the mob should now burst in upon us, break up our meeting and commit violence upon our persons— would this be anything compared with what the slaves endure? No, no: and we [are not] 'as bound with them,' if we shrink in the time of peril, or feel unwilling to sacrifice ourselves, if need be, for their sake."

Harriet Tubman, "Railroad" Conductor

BY WALTER HAZEN

By day we hid and slept. Along the way, there were various stations where we were given food and shelter. A station might be a home or a barn. It might be a church or any other kind of building. The stationmaster was a kindly person who risked much to help us passengers.

By now, you might be thinking we were on some kind of railroad. We weren't. We were traveling along a secret escape route to freedom. In time, this route came to be called the **Underground Railroad**. The brave people who led us from slavery in the South to freedom in the North were called

---

People and Terms to Know

Underground Railroad—secret network by which runaway slaves were led to freedom in the North.

Slaves flee their homes in the South at the beginning of a long journey to freedom in the North by the Underground Railroad.

"conductors." The most famous of these conductors was **Harriet Tubman**. I feel privileged to tell her story.

I first met Harriet in the winter of 1852. I was in a group of ten slaves that she was leading from Maryland to safety in Canada. Along the way, she told us the story of her life. It was a story that made my own problems seem small.

No matter how hard she worked, she couldn't satisfy the overseer of the plantation.

Harriet was born a slave on a plantation in Maryland. She never knew her birth date, but she thought it was around 1820. At the tender age of five, she was put to work. She worked indoors for a while, but she was later sent to the fields. She said she could plow and split wood as well as any slave. But no matter how hard she worked, she couldn't satisfy the overseer of the plantation.

As time passed, Harriet was often beaten. I know now that she was beaten so badly that she had thick scars on her back. Once the overseer even

People and Terms to Know

Harriet Tubman—(c. 1820–1913) most famous "conductor" on the Underground Railroad. She led more than 300 slaves to freedom. Although she never learned to read or write, she became an effective antislavery speaker.

hit her on the head with a lead weight. That blow left her partly deaf and suffering from dizzy spells.

To the overseer of the plantation, Harriet had an "attitude" problem. That is why she was beaten so cruelly. She suffered this treatment until 1849, when she decided to run away. She planned to escape with her two brothers. At the last minute, however, they backed out and refused to go. So Harriet struck out alone. After a journey of 90 miles, she arrived safely in Philadelphia.

Sometime around 1850, Harriet began working for the Underground Railroad. At first, she guided runaway slaves to freedom in the North. Then the **Fugitive Slave Act** changed all that. This was a law that required people to return runaway slaves to their owners. After the law was passed, Harriet and other conductors began taking their "passengers" all the way to Canada.

Each time we stopped to rest and eat at a station, Harriet continued her story. She told us that since joining the Railroad, she had met many important

People and Terms to Know

Fugitive (FYOO•jih•tihv) **Slave Act**—(1850) federal law that said U.S. citizens could be fined and arrested for helping to hide or rescue a runaway (fugitive) slave. The law caused Northerners to hate slavery even more.

◀ Portrait of Harriet Tubman.

abolitionists. One was Frederick Douglass. Mr. Douglass even served for a while as a conductor on the railroad. So did <u>**John Brown**</u>, who was later hanged for his illegal efforts to free slaves.

When each night came, we continued our journey. My group walked the entire way from Maryland to Canada. Some runaways were lucky enough to ride part of the way. Conductors hid them in wagons and carts with false bottoms. How I envied them!

People and Terms to Know

John Brown—(1800–1859) violent abolitionist who killed five proslavery men in Kansas. In 1859, he captured the U.S. arsenal at Harpers Ferry (now in West Virginia) as part of an effort to free slaves. He was hanged in 1859. See the story on page 131.

Absolute silence and cooperation were necessary along the route. Anyone in Harriet's group who whined or complained was certain to face her anger. She carried a pistol and threatened to shoot any runaway who made trouble or thought of turning back. "You'll be free or you'll die!" she warned us.

Our group reached Canada without any problems. Harriet left us there to plan another trip south. Years later, I learned that she made 19 such trips. All told, she led more than three hundred slaves to freedom. On one trip, she brought back her elderly parents. She also managed to rescue her brothers and her sister's family.

Black people called Harriet "**Moses**." They called her this because she was leading slaves to the "Promised Land." You may be familiar with the old **spiritual** "Go Down, Moses." It begins: "Go down, Moses, Way down in Egypt land. Tell ol' Pharaoh, let my people go." Moses is Harriet Tubman, Egypt land is the South, and Pharoah is the slaveowner.

People and Terms to Know

Moses—Hebrew prophet and lawgiver in the Bible who led the Israelites out of slavery in Egypt. Harriet Tubman was known as "Moses" for her role in leading slaves to freedom.

spiritual—religious folksong originally created and sung by black slaves.

Many years after Harriet Tubman led me to freedom, I learned that perhaps as many as fifty thousand slaves had traveled along the Underground Railroad. When war broke out and the Railroad was no longer needed, Harriet continued her fight against slavery. She served in the Union army as a spy, scout, and hospital nurse.

Perhaps as many as fifty thousand slaves had traveled along the Underground Railroad.

After the war, Harriet went to live in Auburn, New York. She opened a home for needy people who had been slaves. It was at this home that I learned to read and write.

Harriet Tubman died on March 10, 1913, having lived to be over 90. My life and the lives of many others were much better because of her.

QUESTIONS TO CONSIDER

1. Why do you think some slaves, like Harriet's two brothers, chose not to try to escape?

2. How did the Fugitive Slave Act change the way the Underground Railroad operated?

3. What do you think you would have done if a runaway slave had knocked on your door at night after the Fugitive Slave Act was passed?

Freedom Train:
The Story of Harriet Tubman
by Dorothy Sterling

Harriet Tubman led so many slaves to freedom that Southern authorities put a price of $40,000 on her head. Reward posters cautioned, "Looks harmless, but she carries a pistol." Dorothy Sterling tells Tubman's exciting and inspiring life story.

Escape from Slavery:
Five Journeys to Freedom
by Doreen Rappaport

Doreen Rappaport presents five true accounts of slaves who escaped to freedom during the time of the Underground Railroad.

Harriet Tubman:
Conductor on the Underground Railroad
by Ann Petry

Ann Petry's biography of Harriet Tubman has become a classic.

The Book That Helped to Start a War

BY JUDITH LLOYD YERO

In the years before the Civil War, many Americans in both the North and the South believed that black people really didn't mind slavery. With her book *Uncle Tom's Cabin*, a woman named **Harriet Beecher Stowe** did more than any person of her time to change that belief.

Stowe never lived in the South. In 1832 she moved to Cincinnati, a city on the northern side of the Ohio River. Across the river was Kentucky, a state where slavery was legal. Many slaves fled into Ohio on their way to freedom. Stowe became a

People and Terms to Know

Harriet Beecher Stowe (stoh)—(1811–1896) author of *Uncle Tom's Cabin*, a book that greatly advanced the cause of abolition. First published as a series in an abolitionist newspaper, the novel sold 300,000 copies when it was published as a book in 1852. It was second only to the Bible in popularity.

UNCLE TOM'S CABIN

Uncle Tom's Cabin continued to be highly popular long after the Civil War.
This 1899 poster advertises a stage play based on the novel.

supporter of the abolitionist movement when she heard their stories.

In her book, Stowe wrote a series of personal stories that showed slaves as human beings with feelings. Her readers could relate to these characters. Her storytelling was so powerful that it stirred great feelings in people. In the North, it helped persuade people that slavery was unjust. Here is the story everyone was talking about.

A slave in Kentucky named **Uncle Tom** and his wife Chloe (KLOH•ee) live and work on a plantation owned by Mr. Shelby. To pay his debts, Shelby is forced to sell Tom and a five-year-old boy named Harry to a white man named Mr. Haley, who is a slave trader. When Harry's mother Eliza learns about the sale, she grabs her son and tells Uncle Tom and his wife that she is going to run away. Chloe urges Tom to escape, too, but he refuses.

Haley discovers that Eliza and Harry have gone and warns Tom not to try to escape. Then Haley goes after Eliza.

People and Terms to Know

Uncle Tom—character in Harriet Beecher Stowe's *Uncle Tom's Cabin*. A hero in the novel, Uncle Tom has come to be an insulting term for a black person who gives in to a white person.

Eliza flees to the Ohio River. It is winter, and the river is filled with chunks of ice. Eliza crosses the river, leaping from one piece of floating ice to another. With Harry in her arms, she finally reaches the Ohio side and freedom.

Enraged that Eliza has escaped, Haley returns to the Shelby Plantation to get the other slave he bought, Uncle Tom. Uncle Tom says a tearful farewell to Chloe, his children, and the other slaves. Then he is led away, his wrists and ankles bound in chains. Young George Shelby, the plantation owner's son, vows someday he will find Tom.

Tom says a tearful farewell to Chloe, his children, and the other slaves.

Haley boards a boat for New Orleans with Tom after buying more slaves, including a mother and her infant son. He sells the child to a stranger on the ship. Rather than live without her child, the mother jumps into the river and drowns.

Even Haley can now see that Tom is a very good man. He realizes that Tom is unlikely to run away, so he takes off the chains. Tom helps the crew whenever he can but spends much of the trip sitting on cotton bales reading his Bible.

On the trip, Tom becomes friendly with a beautiful, golden-haired girl, little Eva, who is traveling with her father. Eva secretly brings Tom and the other slaves candy, oranges, and other treats. Tom carves little toys and trinkets for Eva, who seems to Tom to be like one of the angels in his Bible.

One day, little Eva falls overboard, and Tom leaps into the river to save her. Eva begs her father, Mr. St. Clare, to buy Tom. When he asks Eva why she wants Tom, she replies, "I want to make him happy." St. Clare strikes a deal with Haley, and Tom's life appears a little safer.

When they reach his plantation, St. Clare puts Tom in charge of the horses. St. Clare's wife, Marie, is a sickly and selfish woman. She pays little attention to Eva, so Eva and Tom spend a lot of time together. Marie constantly complains that Eva spends too much time with the slaves. She tells her husband that he should beat the slaves more often, but Tom's influence helps St. Clare to become more Christian.

After several years, little Eva grows ill. Tom's talk of heaven makes her illness a little easier to bear. Eva tells her father that, although she hates the thought of leaving him, she isn't afraid to die. Eva knows her father is good to the slaves, but she fears what will happen to them, and especially to Tom, if her father were to die. She makes St. Clare promise that when she dies, he will free them. Not wanting to admit that he will soon lose his precious daughter, St. Clare agrees.

Eva grows worse. As she is dying, she calls all the slaves to her bedside and gives them each a lock of her hair. She tells them that she is going to heaven and that she wants them to join her there. "You must remember that each one of you can become angels, and be angels forever."

After Eva's death, St. Clare is so filled with sorrow that he can barely think. Without his precious Eva, life isn't worth living. He promises Tom his freedom, but before he can sign the papers, St. Clare dies. Now, Eva's fears come true. Marie is finally able to treat the slaves as she wishes, so she sells Tom to a cruel master, **Simon Legree**.

People and Terms to Know

Simon Legree—character in Harriet Beecher Stowe's *Uncle Tom's Cabin*. He is so fiercely cruel that his name has come to mean "a brutal taskmaster."

Tom continues to work hard, but Legree hates him. When he orders Tom to beat one of the other slaves, Tom refuses. Legree takes out his anger on Tom, beating him severely. This is the first of many beatings Tom suffers at the hands of his cruel, drunken master. Still Tom will not run away. His faith is tested in many ways, but Tom always trusts his Lord. His example of strength and kindness converts many of the other slaves.

His faith is tested in many ways, but Tom always trusts his Lord.

When several slaves escape, Tom admits that he knew their plans, but he refuses to tell Legree where they went. When Legree threatens to kill him, Tom says, "O, Mas'r! don't bring this great sin on your soul! It will hurt you more than 'twill me! Do the worst you can, my troubles'll be over soon; but, if ye don't repent, yours won't never end!" After a moment of silence, Legree, foaming with rage, strikes Tom to the ground.

Several days later, George Shelby, true to his word, comes for Tom. It is too late.

QUESTIONS TO CONSIDER

1. How did Stowe present the slaves in her story?
2. How did she present the slave owners?
3. How do you think Stowe's book helped start the Civil War?

Uncle Tom's Cabin

"A slave warehouse in New Orleans is a house externally not much unlike many others; kept with neatness; and where every day you may see arranged, under a sort of shed along the outside, rows of men and women, who stand there as a sign of the property sold within.

"Then you shall be courteously entreated [begged] to call and examine, and shall find an abundance of husbands, wives, brothers, sisters, fathers, mothers, and young children, to be 'sold separately, or in lots, to suit the convenience of the purchaser;' and that soul immortal, once bought with blood and anguish by the Son of God, . . . can be sold, leased, mortgaged, exchanged for groceries or dry goods, to suit the phases of trade, or the fancy of the purchaser."

The Strength of These Arms: Life in the Slave Quarters
by Raymond Bial

Raymond Bial uses text and photographs to provide a well-rounded introduction to the daily life of slaves in America before the Civil War.

Slavery Time When I Was Chillun
edited by Belinda Hurmence

In 1936, the Library of Congress interviewed more than 2,000 former slaves about their experiences. Belinda Hurmence presents 12 of these oral histories to give a first-hand look at slavery.

To Be a Slave
by Julius Lester

What was it like to be a slave in the South? Award-winning African-American writer Julius Lester uses the actual words of former slaves to create a powerful oral history of slavery.

The Taking of Anthony Burns

BY STEPHEN CURRIE

I am a simple man. I come from a simple family, and I lead a simple life. I am not learned, like the lawyers and judges in the courtroom across the way. I am not wise like the men who make laws, either here in Boston or off in Washington. Their speech is educated. Mine is plain. Their jobs are a great responsibility, while I am only a prison guard. They have the ear of millions, while no one listens to me.

And yet, for all of that, sometimes I think simplicity is best. For proof, I give you young **Anthony Burns** and the way he stood this town—and this nation—on its head.

People and Terms to Know

Anthony Burns—(c. 1834–1862) young man who escaped from slavery in Virginia and went to Boston. In 1854 he was captured by government agents and tried as a runaway slave.

Anthony Burns is led back into slavery in chains through the streets of Boston.

Do you remember the excitement? It all started in 1854, ten years ago, before the start of this terrible Civil War that has caused our nation such distress. I kept the keys for the prison cells, as I do today. I swung shut the gates of each man's cell at the start of his sentence. I swung them wide apart for him at the end. A sorry lot they were—and are—our Boston criminals: pickpockets and burglars, drunkards and fighters, swindlers and murderers. Some get sent here once, others again and again. Some never get out.

The laws held Anthony to be this man's property until the end of time.

Anthony Burns, now, was different. He was a young and weary man, a man with a look of sorrow, a frightened man. I did not know his story at first. I did not know that he was a runaway slave, escaped from his master down in Virginia. I did not know that the laws held Anthony to be this man's property until the end of time, even though he was now in a free state. I was a simple man. To me, Anthony was just another prisoner, though one with a darker skin than most. There are few blacks in Boston today. There were fewer then.

Anthony Burns, I soon learned, had been brought to prison by government **marshals**. They meant to turn him over to his former master, a man named Charles Suttle. Mr. Suttle himself came to Boston to take him home.

You may remember the trial. Mr. Suttle made three arguments before the judge. First, he said, Anthony was his property. The lawyers argued about it, the way lawyers do, and Mr. Suttle's lawyer passed around deeds and titles and all manner of legal papers. They showed that the Suttle family had owned young Anthony since his birth.

Now, I am sure those papers were legal and right and properly signed and sealed. I am a simple man, and I do not understand legal papers, but how is it that a man can own another man? A man may own a horse or a cow, but another man? It makes no sense. I had never thought much about slavery before, but each morning I brought the sad young Anthony Burns out for the trial and each afternoon I locked him back up. I could not help but think that this was a man, not a farm animal, and wonder what gave Mr. Suttle the right to own him.

People and Terms to Know

marshals—law enforcement officials.

Second, Mr. Suttle said that Anthony had escaped from him. It was a crime, escaping, and so Anthony was a criminal. Anthony said he had fallen asleep by accident on a boat, which had then sailed away from slave territory. Mr. Suttle said Anthony had done it on purpose. And again the lawyers argued.

I am not learned like a lawyer. I am a simple man, but I know criminals. I have criminals in my jail. I had them then. I have them now. They are thieves from the streets and toughs from the docks, men who use their fists too soon and their heads too late. Anthony Burns did not belong with them. Each day I thought, "It is not such a bad thing to escape from slavery. It is not so dreadful to run away from misery." I found myself admiring the man's courage and cleverness. I am a simple man, and I could not help but ask why running away from a life of sorrow was such a terrible crime.

And third, Mr. Suttle said, it did not matter that Anthony Burns had reached a free state, Massachusetts, where slavery was not allowed. Anthony still had to be taken back to Virginia. The Fugitive Slave Act said so. This law, I learned, held that a master could force a runaway slave back home, even after he had reached the North. The Southern slaveholders had made that law, but the

Northern lawmakers had agreed to it as well. It was all about preserving the Union, they said, all about keeping the South happy.

I am not a learned man, as I have said, and I do not understand all that politicians say and do. But it seemed to me that the North should not be made to support the South's way of life. And it seemed to me, too, that the law was a wicked law. No one should pull human beings off the street and send them to a lifetime of hard and unpaid labor. Was saving the Union worth such cruelty? Was keeping the South happy so important?

Was saving the Union worth such cruelty? Was keeping the South happy so important?

I was not alone in my thinking. Each day during the trial, the people of Massachusetts gathered near the courtroom. They waved signs and made speeches against sending Anthony Burns back to Virginia. Some were great thinkers—politicians and lawyers and the like. But many were simple men, just like me. They had never thought much about slavery. Most of them had not wanted to meddle in the affairs of the South. They—like me—had changed their minds because of Anthony Burns.

He was so young. Perhaps he was twenty, with a lifetime ahead of him. That lifetime should not have to be spent in slavery.

You remember the trial? The learned, wise judge ordered Anthony Burns sent back to Virginia. Boston abolitionists stormed the courthouse where Burns was being held. Determined to uphold the Fugitive Slave Act, President **Franklin Pierce** ordered the Marines to assist those who guarded Burns. Pierce even ordered a federal ship to return Burns to Virginia. The Act may have been enforced, but 50,000 people stood in protest as Burns was led to the ship.

Then, amazingly, Burns's luck changed. Antislavery men bought him and brought him North. They gave him his freedom. He studied at Oberlin College, became a minister, and moved to Canada. He died two years ago, probably not thirty years old. It was a sorry waste of a life. How much, I ask, was that life cut short by the trial, by weeks in this cold and dank prison, and by the shock of capture by the marshals?

People and Terms to Know

Franklin Pierce—(1804–1869) U.S. statesman, representative, and senator from New Hampshire who became the 14th president of the United States. He served as president from 1853 to 1857.

I am a simple man, and I do not know much, but I do know this: the learned men argued and planned, and all their learning came to nothing. They wrote a law to preserve the Union, and they never asked whether the law was a good one. They let slaveholders make their case in Massachusetts, and they did not think of the effect on Burns himself. They returned Anthony Burns to his master, following the law.

They forgot that we Northerners knew him as a man, not as a slave. All their planning did not keep this nation together and could not avoid this ugly Civil War. They could not even keep Anthony Burns a slave forever.

I would have kept him, kept him here in Boston. He was where he belonged and where he wanted to be. I would have done what was right.

But I am a simple man, and no one listens to me.

QUESTIONS TO CONSIDER

1. How did the case of Anthony Burns change the prison guard's mind about slavery?

2. Why did most citizens of Boston hate the Fugitive Slave Act?

3. How did the Fugitive Slave Act help bring about the Civil War?

4. What in your opinion is Anthony Burns's place in history? Why is his story important?

Anthony Burns:
The Defeat and Triumph of a Fugitive Slave
by Virginia Hamilton

In 1854, Anthony Burns, a fugitive slave from Virginia, was captured in Boston and put on trial. The court's decision to return Burns to his owner outraged thousands of Northerners. Distinguished African-American author Virginia Hamilton tells the moving story of Burns's struggle to be free.

The Antislavery Movement
by James T. Rogers

James T. Rogers presents a thorough account of the opposition to slavery in America from its beginnings.

Amistad: A Long Road to Freedom
by Walter Dean Myers

In 1840, a group of Africans who had rebelled on a slave ship, Amistad, were put on trial. Would the rebellious Africans be sent to slavery in Cuba or set free? Walter Dean Myers tells the exciting story of "the Amistad affair."

Steps Toward War

Gold, Slavery, and Henry Clay

BY JUDITH LLOYD YERO

On a January morning in 1848, James W. Marshall was inspecting work on a sawmill. He and his men were building it for California landowner John Sutter. A reflection from the bottom of the newly built **millrace** caught his eye. Reaching into the water, Marshall plucked a shiny bit of metal the size of a pea from the streambed.

Less than two months later, a small article appeared in a San Francisco paper, the *Californian*.

> **Gold Mine Found.** In the newly made raceway of the Saw Mill recently erected by Captain Sutter on the American fork, gold has been

---

People and Terms to Know

millrace—channel for the water that drives a mill wheel. Also called a raceway.

Henry Clay addresses the Senate during the debate on the Compromise of 1850.

found in considerable quantities. One person brought thirty dollars worth to New Helvetica [Sacramento], gathered there in a short time. California, no doubt, is rich in mineral wealth, great chance here for scientific capitalists.

The writer of the article didn't know beforehand the speed with which the "**capitalists**" changed the face of California and, indeed, the nation itself. By May, the *Californian* itself was forced to stop its presses. "The majority of our subscribers and many of our advertisers have closed their doors and places of business and left town. . . ." The California **gold rush** was on.

By August, 4,000 miners had scattered their tents across the hillsides near the American River. Thousands of other hopeful **prospectors** headed for California. Some sailed around Cape Horn at the tip of South America. Others joined the wagons making the dangerous 2,000-mile trip across the country. By the end of 1849, less than 22 months after the newspaper article, the population of California had increased by 80,000 people.

People and Terms to Know

capitalists (KAP•ih•tihl•ihsts)—people who lay out money (capital) for something expected to make a profit.

gold rush—rapid movement of many people to a region where gold has been discovered.

prospectors—people who explore an area for mineral deposits like gold or oil.

With the rapid growth in population, the need for a better government became urgent. Even before the discovery of gold, California had asked to become a **territory**. Taking matters into their own hands, Californians quickly adopted a constitution and sent two representatives to Congress to present their case. They were no longer satisfied with being a territory. Now, they were demanding immediate statehood! Most important, the California constitution forbade slavery.

> *Most important, the California constitution forbade slavery.*

The arguments over slavery had been raging for years. It was Washington policy to keep the number of slave and free states equal so that their power was balanced in the Senate. After Texas became a state in 1845, there were 28 states—15 slave states and 13 free states. Over the next several years, Iowa and Wisconsin were admitted. Since they did not allow slavery, once again the balance was restored. California would tip the balance toward antislavery, something the South would not allow.

People and Terms to Know

territory—part of the United States that is not a state but that has a governor and a legislature.

A breakup of the Union was a strong threat. Some Californians, disgusted with the delay in Washington, threatened to set up a new country. They would call it the **Bear Flag Republic**.

Tensions were running high when Henry Clay, who had represented Kentucky in Congress for nearly forty years, worked out a compromise. Clay had plenty of experience keeping both sides happy. He had put together compromises throughout his career.

Clay did not approve of slavery, but he believed that keeping the Union together was more important. In early 1850, Clay addressed Congress. He said that it was "desirable, for the peace, concord, and harmony of the Union of these States, to settle . . . all existing questions of controversy between them arising out of . . . slavery upon a fair, equitable and just basis."

Clay offered a set of proposals for what is now called the **Compromise of 1850**. The proposals included admitting California as a free state.

People and Terms to Know

Bear Flag Republic—nation proclaimed by American settlers in California when they declared independence from Mexico in 1846.

Compromise of 1850—series of laws meant to settle the disagreements between free states and slave states.

Also, Clay proposed that the people in the new territories of New Mexico and Utah would decide when they applied for statehood whether they wanted to be free or slave states.

Another proposal let slavery continue in Washington, D.C., but ended the huge slave market that existed in the city.

All citizens were required to help capture and return escaped slaves to their owners.

Finally, to satisfy the Southern states, Clay included the Fugitive Slave Act. This part of the Compromise caused the most heated arguments. For many years, antislavery Northerners had helped runaway slaves escape to the North and Canada. The Underground Railroad may have helped up to fifty thousand slaves escape between 1830 and 1860.

According to the Fugitive Slave Act, all citizens were required to help capture and return escaped slaves to their owners. Special government officers decided whether the person was really someone's slave. These officers received a payment of $5 if a person was let go. They received $10 for every slave returned to an owner. Thus, these officers were rewarded for deciding in a slave owner's favor. Even worse, there was no protection for blacks who were not slaves.

The Compromise was eventually passed. However, it added fuel to the fires that would eventually cause the Union to split. The harshness of the Fugitive Slave Act brought the issue of slavery home to many Northerners who had not been affected by the issues before. Nine Northern states passed "personal liberty laws" declaring that they wouldn't cooperate with the federal government. The Underground Railroad reached its highest peak of activity. Abolitionists became even more resolved to end slavery.

Henry Clay died in 1852. He was spared from seeing the breakup of the Union that he had worked so hard to prevent. James W. Marshall could never have guessed that the pea-sized bit of gold he found in a California stream would start a gold rush that ended in California statehood. Nor could he have predicted that the state's decision about slavery would result in a compromise that would rock the nation. In the late 1800s, a French writer describing the history of California said, "It was the gold of California that gave the fatal blow to the institution of slavery in the United States."

QUESTIONS TO CONSIDER

1. Why do you think the discovery of gold in California made the residents eager to gain statehood?

2. What is the Compromise of 1850 and what was its purpose?

3. Why did Henry Clay propose the Fugitive Slave Act?

4. What did the French writer mean when he said the discovery of gold in California "gave the fatal blow to the institution of slavery in the United States"?

Gold Fever:
Tales from the California Gold Rush
by Rosalyn Schanzer

In January 1848, gold was discovered in California. Word of the discovery traveled around the world with lightning speed, prompting a wild gold rush. Rosalyn Schanzer uses firsthand reports of how the gold-seekers got to California and what they did when they arrived.

The Man Who Wouldn't Give Up:
Henry Clay
by Katherine Elliot Wilkie

Henry Clay was a stubborn man. He ran for president unsuccessfully several times and he kept putting together compromises between the free states and the slave states to keep the Union from coming apart. Katherine Elliot Wilkie tells his story.

The Westward Movement and
Abolitionism, 1815–1850
by William Loren Katz

William Loren Katz examines the effect that American westward expansion had on the antislavery movement.

John Brown: Martyr or Murderer?

BY MARIANNE McCOMB

A small group of men watched and waited as the sun disappeared over the rim of the Kansas prairie. A cool, damp wind blew through the tall grasses and rippled the waters of Pottawatomie Creek. The wind chilled the men and made their wait uncomfortable.

They stayed crouched in their hiding place in the brush along the creek until nearly ten o'clock at night. Finally, under the cover of complete darkness, the group got up and waded across the creek to the small log cabin on the northern shore.

The men moved in complete silence. Their mission was a dangerous one. They knew they would be shot on sight if they were spotted. Slowly they crept up to the front door of the cabin. Two

Thomas Hovenden's painting *The Last Moments of John Brown* presents the violent abolitionist as a loving old man.

growling dogs blocked their way, but the men kicked them aside. Then the leader of the group, an old man in dirty clothes and a torn straw hat, banged furiously on the cabin door.

After a moment, a man from inside the cabin opened the door. Silently, he raised his lantern a little higher so that he could see the faces of the men who had come knocking. With an angry shout, the leader of the group shoved him aside and burst into the cabin.

John Brown's **massacre** at Pottawatomie Creek had begun.

*   *   *

The man who opened the door to John Brown that night was James P. Doyle, a poor white man from Tennessee who had recently settled in the Pottawatomie region of Kansas. The **Kansas-Nebraska Act** of 1854 had brought many new

---

People and Terms to Know

massacre (MAS•uh•kuhr)—killing of a group of people in an especially cruel way.

Kansas–Nebraska Act—(1854) law that established the Kansas and Nebraska territories and opened them for settlement. Residents would vote to decide whether their future states would be free or slave. Eventually, Kansas became a breeding ground for the Civil War because the North and the South each tried to send the most settlers into the new territory.

people to the territory. Like many of his neighbors, Doyle was strongly for slavery. In the spring of 1856, he had joined hundreds of others in a fight to make slavery legal in Kansas. These men promised to search every town and valley of the state and drive out any abolitionist they could find. When that was done, they would be able to open the Kansas borders to slave trading.

These men promised to search every town and valley of the state and drive out any abolitionist they could find.

By late spring, six Kansas abolitionists had been brutally murdered. On May 21, 1856, the same proslavery men stormed and burned the town of Lawrence, Kansas. They said it was a "nest" of abolitionists.

Many Kansans were upset about the burning of Lawrence. Angriest of all, perhaps, was John Brown, who had long hated anything and everything having to do with slavery.

Brown was born in Torrington, Connecticut, on May 9, 1800. He was a thin and serious child, the third of six children born to Owen and Ruth Brown. The Browns filled their small Connecticut house with religion. They taught their children to "fear

God and keep His commandments" in their hearts. The Browns also taught their children not to hate blacks. They said that slavery was a sin against God.

When he was a young man, John Brown married a pretty woman named Dianthe. Dianthe helped soothe John whenever he had one of his many outbursts of temper. On July 25, 1821, Dianthe gave birth to their first child, John Brown, Jr.

A little over ten years later, Dianthe died after giving birth to their seventh child. Brown buried mother and child and promised himself that he would look after his family any way he could.

A year later, Brown remarried. His new wife, Mary Ann, also was able to jolly Brown out of his many bad moods.

The question of slavery made Brown very angry. He believed all slaves should be set free. He kept up-to-date on the growing antislavery movement in the North. He attended antislavery meetings whenever he could. Often, he left these meetings furious about the way blacks were being treated.

After the explosive Kansas–Nebraska Act had passed in the Senate, Brown made plans to move to Kansas. Five of his sons had already settled on the banks of Pottawatomie Creek. The Brown boys had written to their father and begged him to come. They needed help fighting the people who wanted to make Kansas a slave state.

O ver a year later, Brown moved to Kansas. Almost at once, he became caught up in the anti-slavery movement and spoke his mind whenever he could. Before long, Brown became known as an angry abolitionist.

He said that it was time to "fight fire with fire."

The burning of the town of Lawrence took place soon after Brown arrived in Kansas. Sick to death of the men and women who supported slavery, Brown declared it was time to seek revenge. Moving quickly, he gathered as many antislavery friends and neighbors as he could find. He said that it was time to "fight fire with fire" and "strike terror in the hearts of the proslavery people." It was John Brown, along with four of his sons and three neighbors, who arrived at the door of James Doyle late on the night of May 24, 1856.

* * *

When Brown and the others pushed their way into Doyle's cabin, Doyle's wife began to moan in fear. She pulled her little girl toward her and tried to shield her three sons with her own body. "I told you what you were going to get," she screamed at her husband, who stood rigid with fear. Brown announced that "the Northern Army had come." Then he and his men dragged her husband and two of her sons out into the windy night.

As soon as they had their prisoners clear of the cabin, Brown's group fell on the three and began hacking at them with their short swords. Although the three prisoners tried to fight back, they were outnumbered. Within minutes, the three Doyles were dead, and their blood was spreading across the hard-packed dirt of the Kansas prairie.

Brown and his men left the Doyles where they lay and began moving south along the Pottawatomie. Their next stop was at a cabin owned by a man named Wilkinson. Like Doyle, Wilkinson had a reputation as a proslavery fighter. Brown knocked on Wilkinson's door and pretended to be lost. When Wilkinson opened the door and stepped out into the black night, Brown and his men grabbed him.

Ignoring the screams of the Wilkinson family, Brown gave the order for his men to take their prisoner away. Brown's followers dragged Wilkinson 150 yards from the cabin and then slit open his throat.

Dawn was fast approaching by the time Brown and his group finished murdering Wilkinson. Moving quickly now, the small group made their way to James Harris's cabin on Pottawatomie Creek. Without hesitating, Brown and the others broke into Harris's house and found the man fast asleep in bed with his wife and child. Three men who were spending the night at Harris's house lay sleeping nearby.

Brown ordered the four men to rise and questioned them carefully. He needed to find out which were proslavery. Harris and two others managed to convince Brown that they were peaceful citizens of Kansas. Brown sent the fourth man, William Sherman, to wait outside. He knew that Sherman had been deeply involved in the fight to legalize slavery in Kansas.

After he finished questioning the men, Brown made his way outside. He leaned against the cabin wall and watched for a signal from his sons. After a short wait, he heard a whistle. Without a backward glance, Brown turned away from the house and began walking back to his camp. Behind him, in the murky waters of the Pottawatomie, lay the mangled body of William Sherman. He had been hacked to death in the name of keeping slavery out of Kansas.

*   *   *

On that bloody night in 1856, Brown and his group killed five people who had been fighting to legalize slavery in Kansas. He said that these five deaths were payback for the deaths of the six Kansas abolitionists. As word spread of the attacks, other violent men copied them. In all, some 200 people were murdered.

As word spread of the attacks, other violent men copied them.

A little over three years after the massacre at Pottawatomie Creek, Brown planned a raid on the federal arsenal at Harpers Ferry. He said that once he had grabbed the arsenal, slaves in the South would join him and form an "army of emancipation."

Portrait of John Brown. ▶

On October 16, Brown and his men took control of the arsenal and took nearly sixty **hostages**. Some thirty-six hours later, Brown was captured by a small force of the U.S. Marines. Two of his sons were killed, and Brown himself was wounded. Later that same year, Brown was tried and convicted of **treason** in Virginia. He was hanged on December 2, 1859. Many abolitionists called him a martyr (MAHR•tuhr) because he had given his life for the antislavery movement.

People and Terms to Know

hostages (HAHS•tihj•uhs)—people held as prisoners until some demands are agreed to.
treason—high crime of betrayal of or disloyalty to one's country.

1. How would you describe John Brown?

2. Why was Kansas the scene of so much bloodshed?

3. How do you feel about John Brown's actions at Pottawatomie Creek?

3. Why might people say that John Brown was partially responsible for bringing about the Civil War?

Primary Source

John Brown's Speech to the Court

After John Brown was sentenced to death, he addressed a final speech to the court.

"I believe that to have interfered as I have done—as I have always freely admitted I have done—in behalf of [God's] despised poor, was not wrong but right. Now if it is deemed necessary that I should forfeit my life for the furtherance of the ends of justice and mingle my blood with the blood of my children and with the blood of millions in this slave country, whose rights are disregarded by wicked, cruel, and unjust enactments [laws]—I submit; so let it be done!"

Blood on the Senate Floor

BY DEE MASTERS

In 1856, the U.S. Congress had to decide whether Kansas would be a free state or a slave state when it entered the Union. Things there had become very bad. After the 1854 Kansas-Nebraska Act had allowed slavery in the territory, many supporters of slavery moved to Kansas. Two different governments were set up, one in favor of slavery, the other against it. There was so much rioting and bloodshed, people were calling it "Bleeding Kansas." This was the situation when the Senate began its debates.

United States President Franklin Pierce supported those who were for slavery in Kansas.

This 1856 cartoon shows Preston Brooks attacking Charles Sumner at his desk in the Senate.

Stephen A. Douglas, the senator from Illinois, supported a plan that would let settlers vote on whether their state would be slave or free. Late in the debate, Massachusetts Senator **Charles Sumner** took the floor. He had memorized his whole 112-page speech. On May 19, 1856, at one o'clock in the afternoon, Charles Sumner began.

"Mr. President, . . . seldom in the history of nations has such a question been presented. A crime has been committed, which is without example in the records of the past."

Sumner spoke for three hours, exposing "the Crime Against Kansas." He attacked President Pierce for allowing it. He said Stephen Douglas's ideas had put slavery in Kansas. The next day Sumner continued. He wanted to admit Kansas immediately as a free state.

People and Terms to Know

Stephen A. Douglas—(1813–1861) famed public speaker who served both as representative and senator from Illinois. Lincoln debated Douglas when he ran for Douglas's Senate seat.

Charles Sumner—(1811–1874) Republican senator from Massachusetts (1851–1874). He opposed slavery and the Fugitive Slave Act and favored the right of blacks to vote.

The speech drew a huge audience from both houses of Congress. Sumner's attack on slavery was no surprise. What did surprise many was that Sumner got personal. He said some of the Southern senators had "raised themselves" to importance by supporting "human wrongs."

He especially attacked Senator Andrew P. Butler, who came from the slave state of South Carolina. Southern senators immediately said Sumner's speech was full of "gross insults." Proslavery Senator Douglas asked whether he was trying to get them so angry they would "kick him as we would a dog in the street." Even Sumner's friends thought he had gone too far. They worried for his personal safety.

He said some of the Southern senators had "raised themselves" to importance by supporting "human wrongs."

Preston S. Brooks, a congressman from South Carolina, was especially upset. Senator Butler was his uncle! The thirty-six-year-old Brooks was a likable man. He was moderate in politics and a

---

People and Terms to Know

Preston S. Brooks—(1819–1857) U.S. representative from South Carolina (1852–1857) who attacked Senator Charles Sumner in the Senate after Sumner's verbal attack on his uncle Andrew P. Butler.

veteran of the **Mexican War**. However, he was proud of the South and his state. He hated abolitionists and was loyal to his family.

Gentlemen in the South had a code of honor. When a man was insulted, he should not take it lying down. He should whip the offending person. Brooks's uncle was elderly. Brooks felt it was his duty to step in and punish Sumner for his insults to Butler and to South Carolina.

Brooks said he thought about whether he should use "a horsewhip or a cowhide," but believed that Sumner was stronger than he was and might take it from him. That, he said, would have forced him to do something that he would have regretted for the rest of his life. "It was expressly to avoid taking life that I used an ordinary cane."

He chose a cane with a gold head. Brooks hunted for Sumner for two days, telling other Southern congressmen of his plan. On the third day, Brooks waited in the Senate lobby. At a quarter of

---

People and Terms to Know

Mexican War—(1846–1848) war between Mexico and the United States. The war began after Mexico refused to accept U.S. annexation of Texas in 1845. After winning the war, the United States acquired Mexican territory from the Rio Grande to the Pacific coast.

one, the Senate quit work early. Most of the senators left, but Sumner stayed at his desk.

Brooks sat in a desk at the back of the Senate. Several other Southern senators, knowing of Brooks's plan, stayed near. Brooks got up and went to Sumner's desk. With formal politeness Brooks said, "Mr. Sumner."

Sumner glanced up. He had no idea who Brooks was.

Brooks continued, "I have read your speech twice over carefully. It is a **libel** on South Carolina and Mr. Butler, who is a relative of mine."

Sumner started to stand, and Brooks hit him with the cane. Sumner threw out his arms to protect himself. Brooks later said he felt "compelled to strike him harder than I had intended." He struck Sumner over and over on the head, later bragging, "Every lick went where I intended."

Sumner was trapped behind his Senate desk, which was bolted to the floor. Blood was running into his eyes. With a mighty effort he rose up, ripping out the bolts that held the desk to the floor. He staggered forward, dazed and unable to see. Brooks continued to beat him.

People and Terms to Know

libel (LY•buhl)—crime of making damaging or false statements about a person.

The cane snapped, and Brooks continued to strike with the head of the cane. Sumner staggered away. When he finally started to fall, Brooks held him up with one hand while beating him with the other. At this point, Brooks hit Sumner at least thirty more times with the head of the cane.

> *The cane snapped, and Brooks continued to strike with the head of the cane.*

All of this happened quickly. As fast as he could reach him, Senator John Crittenden from Kentucky grabbed Brooks and pulled him away, saying he didn't approve "of such violence in the Senate chamber. Don't kill him."

Brooks, realizing he had hurt Sumner more than he had meant to, replied, "I did not intend to kill him, but I did intend to whip him."

Representative Keitt from Brooks's home state charged down the aisle with his own cane lifted above his head, shouting, "Let them alone!"

Senator Robert Toombs of Georgia kept Keitt from striking the Kentucky senator. He had done nothing to help stop Brooks's attack on Sumner. He later said, "I approved it."

Senator Stephen A. Douglas was in the hall too. But even though Sumner had attacked him for selling out to slave interests, he did not join the brawl. He said he was afraid of being misunderstood.

Brooks was taken to a small room where a cut he had received from his own cane was washed. Then he left. A friend of Sumner's had entered in time to catch Sumner and ease him to the floor. According to the *Congressional Globe*, Sumner lay "as senseless as a corpse for several minutes"; his head was bleeding heavily, and blood covered his clothes.

Sumner came to, said he could walk, and asked that his papers be put away. Leaning on friends, he was helped to a side room. A doctor was called, but he could not tell how seriously Sumner was hurt. Taken home and stripped of his blood-soaked clothes, Sumner whispered, "I could not believe that a thing like this was possible."

Brooks was arrested, but he was freed on bail. After a long, bitter debate, the House of Representatives voted 121 to 95 to expel him. It was not the two-thirds vote necessary. Brooks remained. He was eventually fined $300.

The South made Brooks a hero. Southerners in Washington talked of "cutting the throats of every abolitionist." Brooks was sent several new canes. On one was written, "Hit him again."

In the North, crowds gathered in cities to support Sumner. They called Brooks's attack "a crime against the right of free speech and the dignity of a free state." Lillian R. Clark, then a Connecticut schoolgirl, told her parents, "I don't think it is very much use to stay any longer in High School, as the boys would better be learning to hold muskets, and the girls to make bullets."

Sumner was reelected to the Senate. But his Senate chair remained empty for three years, as he tried to get his health back. At the time of the attack, Sumner was a member of a new political party— the Republican party. It had one driving goal, to end slavery. Sumner was one of the first Republicans. The first successful Republican presidential candidate was Abraham Lincoln. In many ways, the blows to Charles Sumner were the first struck in the Civil War.

QUESTIONS TO CONSIDER

1. What was the problem in Kansas that the senators were debating?

2. What is your opinion of Charles Sumner's attack on slavery?

3. Why did Preston Brooks believe it was right for him to attack Senator Sumner?

4. What part of the story affects you the most? Why?

Dred Scott and the Supreme Court's Terrible Decision

BY JUDY VOLEM

Sarah's Wisconsin kitchen was filled with wonderful smells coming from a bubbling soup pot. A nearly finished quilt was spread out on the table. Ruth glanced at Sarah's work and then got up to put more wood in the stove's firebox. Ruth had been helping her friend Sarah stitch together squares all morning.

Sarah reached into her bag of fabric scraps. She was looking for the perfect piece to finish the last quilt square. Sarah called it a freedom quilt because it celebrated her family's release from slavery. She looked at the numbers she had stitched on the bottom corner of the quilt. That year, 1857, marked the date two years ago that she and her husband had finally saved enough money to buy their freedom.

FRANK LESLIE'S
ILLUSTRATED
NEWSPAPER

Entered according to Act of Congress, in the year 1857, by FRANK LESLIE, in the Clerk's Office of the District Court for the Southern District of New York. (Copyrighted June 27, 1857.)

[No. 82.—VOL. IV.]   NEW YORK, SATURDAY, JUNE 27, 1857.   [PRICE 6 CENTS.

TO TOURISTS AND TRAVELLERS.

We shall be happy to receive personal narratives, of land or sea, including adventures and incidents, from every person who pleases to correspond with our paper.

We take this opportunity of returning our thanks to our numerous artistic correspondents throughout the country, for the many sketches we are constantly receiving from them of the news of the day. We trust they will spare no pains to furnish us with drawings of events as they may occur. We would also remind them that it is necessary to send all sketches, if possible, by the earliest conveyance.

VISIT TO DRED SCOTT—HIS FAMILY—INCIDENTS OF HIS LIFE—DECISION OF THE SUPREME COURT.

WHILE standing in the Fair grounds at St. Louis, and engaged in conversation with a prominent citizen of that enterprising city, he suddenly asked us if we would not like to be introduced to Dred Scott. Upon expressing a desire to be thus honored, the gentleman called to an old negro who was standing near by, and our wish was gratified. Dred made a rude obeisance to our recognition, and seemed to enjoy the notice we expended upon him. We found him on examination to be a pure-blooded African, perhaps fifty years of age, with a shrewd, intelligent, good-natured face, of rather light frame, being not more than five feet six inches high. After some general remarks we expressed a wish to get his portrait (we had made

ELIZA AND LIZZIE, CHILDREN OF DRED SCOTT.

efforts before, through correspondents, and failed), and asked him if he would not go to Fitzgibbon's gallery and

have it taken. The gentleman present explained to Dred that it was proper he should have his likeness in the "great illustrated paper of the country," overruled his many objections, which seemed to grow out of a superstitious feeling, and he promised to be at the gallery the next day. This appointment Dred did not keep. Determined not to be foiled, we sought an interview with Mr. Crane, Dred's lawyer, who promptly gave us a letter of introduction, explaining to Dred that it was to his advantage to have his picture taken to be engraved for our paper, and also directions where we could find his domicile. We found the place with difficulty, the streets in Dred's neighborhood being more clearly defined in the plan of the city than on the mother earth; we finally reached a wooden house, however, protected by a balcony that answered the description. Approaching the door, we saw a smart, tidy-looking negress, perhaps thirty years of age, who, with two female assistants, was busy ironing. To our question, "Is this where Dred Scott lives?" we received, rather hesitatingly, the answer, "Yes." Upon our asking if he was home, she said,

"What white man arter dad nigger fur?—why don't white man 'tend to his own business, and let dat nigger 'lone? Some of dese days dey'll steal dat nigger—dat are a fact."

Sarah pulled out a scrap of red cotton patterned with white pinwheels.

"Who did that belong to, Sarah?" Ruth asked. "It looks like it's from a dress."

"This piece has been resting here in my bag for nearly twenty years. That's how long it's been since Harriet Scott left the Wisconsin Territory. It's from her favorite dress. She must have worn it every Sunday until she finally wore it out."

Sarah sighed as she remembered Harriet. They had had a lot in common. Both of them had been born slaves in the South. They had left their childhood homes when their masters' families had moved to the Wisconsin Territory.

"I believe that Harriet wore the red pinwheel dress to her wedding too," Sarah said. "I felt like I had gained an older brother when Harriet married **Dred Scott**. He was such a nice man. He was born in Virginia and was a slave of a man named Peter Blow. Dred was bought by Dr. John Emerson, a doctor in the Army. Dred moved with Dr. Emerson

---

People and Terms to Know

Dred Scott—(c. 1795–1858) American slave born in Virginia. He sued for his freedom after living for four years with his master in states where slavery had been banned by the Missouri Compromise. After a long court fight, the U. S. Supreme Court ruled in 1857 that he was not a citizen and was still a slave. The Missouri Compromise was declared unconstitutional.

from St. Louis, Missouri, to Illinois and then to Wisconsin. Harriet married Dred in 1836 when her owner agreed to sell her to Dr. Emerson.

"It was against the law to buy and sell slaves here, north of Missouri," Sarah continued, "but that didn't stop people from bringing slaves with them from the South. Did you ever hear of the **Missouri Compromise**?"

"Seems like I did hear about that," said Ruth. "That was a law that made Missouri a slave state."

"That's right," Sarah said, "and slavery was not legal in Wisconsin, according to the Compromise. Well, we all talked about being free. It was a dream we all shared. Even then I was planning to buy my freedom. I was saving money from the laundry that I took in."

"Did the Scotts stay in Wisconsin Territory?" asked Ruth.

"Only for a while," Sarah replied. "Dr. Emerson moved back to Missouri when he married. He left Harriet and Dred behind for a time. I tried to talk

---

People and Terms to Know

Missouri Compromise—(1820) law providing for the admission of Maine as a free state and Missouri as a slave state.

them into running away, but they seemed content at the time and felt safe. When Dr. Emerson sent for them in 1838, they left the free territory. They traveled down the Mississippi River to meet their master in St. Louis. That was the last time I saw them.

"I heard about Harriet and Dred from people who moved up here from Missouri. That was after Wisconsin became a state in 1848. I learned of the births of their daughters, Eliza and Lizzie."

Sarah went on to tell Ruth how things had changed when Dr. Emerson died. His widow moved to New York and left the Scotts in the South. Although their owner was gone, Dred still labored for others. He was rented out like a work animal.

Sarah shook her head sadly as she continued her story. "Dred must have longed for freedom when he looked at his small daughters and thought of the lives they would lead. He tried to buy his family's freedom from Dr. Emerson's widow, but she refused. That's when Dred finally did something else to try to gain his freedom."

Sarah started to cut the red cloth into triangles as she went on with her story. "Dred had learned a thing or two from living in the North. He knew some folks in the South who would help him. Those folks didn't want to see slavery spread into the new states. You remember I mentioned Peter Blow?" Ruth nodded.

"Well, Peter Blow had a son, Taylor. He helped Dred sue in court to gain his freedom."

"What happened then?" asked Ruth, as she got up to stir the soup.

"Harriet sent me a news clipping from the first trial in Missouri in 1846. Dred claimed that he was a free person because he had lived in the free state of Illinois and in the Wisconsin Territory, where slavery was against the law. He lost, and his lawyers appealed to have his case heard again. This went on for ten long years until it finally reached the **U.S. Supreme Court**.

"My sister told me about Harriet around 1852. The Scott family was struggling. Dred was becoming famous, but that didn't make life any easier. The state supreme court in Missouri ruled that the family became slaves when they returned to Missouri."

"Then what happened to them?" Ruth asked.

"A terrible decision. Terrible," Sarah murmured. "Wait. I'll show you what I mean."

People and Terms to Know

U.S. Supreme Court—highest court in the United States. Nine judges are nominated by the president with the "advice and consent" of the Senate. The judges serve for life. The role of the court is to see that the people's rights, according to the Constitution, are protected.

Sarah left the room. When she returned, she had a faded newspaper article dated March 1857. As Sarah read the article aloud, Ruth understood what Sarah had meant. She gasped as she realized that the ruling by the Supreme Court in Washington affected her and all black people.

Dred Scott was still a slave and would be a slave wherever he went. He was property, and he had no rights. Chief Justice **Roger B. Taney** said that people whose ancestors were African were not citizens and had no rights.

> *Dred Scott was still a slave and would be a slave wherever he went.*

"Oh, my. What happened to Dred?" asked Ruth.

"Well, Peter Blow's son, Taylor, finally bought his freedom. Dred worked as a porter in a St. Louis hotel and died of tuberculosis in 1858. Someone told me that Dred Scott said that the case had brought him a 'heap of trouble' and if he had realized how long it would last, he never would have started it."

People and Terms to Know

Roger B. Taney (TAW•nee)—(1777–1864) chief justice of the U.S. Supreme Court from 1836 to 1864. Taney was born in Maryland to a wealthy Southern family. He held strong proslavery views. He wrote the majority opinion in the *Dred Scott* case. In addition to stating that people of African descent were not citizens, he wrote that the states had the power to decide whether a person was a slave. This meant that the Missouri Compromise was no longer valid, so Congress could not outlaw slavery in new territories.

"What does this mean for us?" Ruth asked.

Sarah spread her hand gently across her freedom quilt.

"It means," she replied sadly, "that we still have a long way to go before we will be truly free."

QUESTIONS TO CONSIDER

1. Why did Dred Scott believe the courts would give him his freedom?

2. In what other ways could a slave gain freedom?

3. What is your opinion of the *Dred Scott* decision?

4. How did this decision help push the nation toward civil war?

The Dred Scott Decision
by Brendan January

The Dred Scott case aroused fierce passions and helped drive the North and South further apart. Brendan January presents a clear account of the background and the issues in this landmark Supreme Court case.

The Dred Scott Case: Testing the Right to Live Free
by Jennifer Fleischner

Jennifer Fleischner examines the issues—including presidential politics—that served as context for the Dred Scott case.

Roger Taney: The Dred Scott Legacy
by Suzanne Freedman

Suzanne Freedman profiles Chief Justice Roger B. Taney, who wrote the majority opinion in the landmark Dred Scott case.

Mary Boykin Chesnut: A Born Rebel

BY WALTER HAZEN

I have just read the diary of **Mary Boykin Chesnut**. It is a wonderful book. It was written by a woman who had a close-up view of the events in the South that led to war and of the war itself. It is written as a diary.

Mary Boykin Miller came from a wealthy, powerful family in South Carolina. Her father had served in both houses of Congress. In the 1820s, he was the governor of South Carolina. That was when the country was in a big fuss over tariffs, and

---

People and Terms to Know

Mary Boykin Chesnut—(1823–1886) South Carolinian whose diary provides an excellent picture of life in the South during the Civil War.

Portrait of Mary Chesnut and her husband James.

<u>John C. Calhoun</u> was arguing that states could over-rule federal laws. People were saying that if the federal government didn't let a state **nullify** a federal law, the state had the right to leave the union. Mary's family felt very strongly that Calhoun was right. No wonder Mary was, as she said, "of necessity a 'rebel born.'"

Mary was given a fine education at a boarding school in Charleston, South Carolina. When she was 14, she fell madly in love with James Chesnut, son of one of the wealthiest landowners in the state. He was 23. They married when she was 17. Mary's life thereafter centered on her husband. They never had any children, and she gave her time and energies to his career. Whether as plantation owner, South Carolina lawmaker, United States senator, aide to President **Jefferson Davis**, or officer in the Confederate army, James Chesnut could count on his wife being at his side.

People and Terms to Know

John C. Calhoun—(1782–1850) statesman from South Carolina who pushed the idea of states' rights. He is best known for the nullification theory, which held that, under the Constitution, a state had the right to cancel a federal law that was harmful to it.

nullify (NUHL•uh•fy)—make it have no legal force.

Jefferson Davis—(1808–1889) only president of the Confederate States of America. He was charged with treason after the Civil War and imprisoned for two years.

While Mary Boykin Chesnut might have been a "rebel born," she did not share the common view about slavery. Mary considered herself an abolitionist. In one of her early diary entries, she wrote that, in her opinion, slavery was both wrong and a sin. On the other hand, Mary's view that the slaves themselves were uncivilized Africans was very common.

In her opinion, slavery was both wrong and a sin.

Mary also had mixed feelings about the act that led directly to war between the North and the South. I refer, of course, to South Carolina leaving the Union. Mary had followed events closely during those years when her father was governor and later when her husband was a United States senator. She supported South Carolina's move. She nevertheless wrote in early December 1860 that she was afraid to see her state break with so great a power as the United States.

About five weeks earlier, she had written:

"It was while I was in Florida, on November 11th, that my husband resigned his seat in the Senate of the United States. [He returned to South Carolina to help prepare the state for secession.] I might not have been able to influence him, but I should have tried."

Yet, she later wrote that she was ready and willing to secede. Her reason was that South Carolina had been angry for years. She felt that it was time for people to "fight and stop talking." She believed in a state's right to quit the Union if it believed it was justified in doing so.

Mary Boykin Chesnut described the pride and excitement people felt in the days before the first shots of the Civil War were fired.

"While we were in Camden [a city northeast of South Carolina's capital, Columbia], we were busy with excitement, drilling, marching, arming, and wearing blue **cockades**."

Back in Charleston the night before **Fort Sumter** was fired on, she wrote:

"Yesterday was the merriest, maddest dinner we have had yet." Everyone, she said, did their best to be wise and witty.

People and Terms to Know

cockades—knots of ribbon worn on hats as part of a military uniform.

Fort Sumter—Union fort at Charleston, South Carolina. In 1861, South Carolina requested that the commander of the fort surrender. The commander agreed to do so when his supplies ran out. Aware that new supplies were on the way, South Carolina refused his offer. On April 12, 1861, South Carolinian troops fired on the fort, and the Civil War started.

And so it went in those last few hours of peace. Excitement was mixed with concern and worry. Mary Chesnut's husband was, at that time, a colonel on the staff of **General Beauregard**. He was given the responsibility to row out to Fort Sumter and demand that the fort surrender to the Confederate government. In her diary entry of April 12, she wrote: "I do not pretend to go to sleep. How can I? If **Anderson** does not accept terms [to surrender] at four o'clock, the orders are he shall be fired upon."

And a little later: "I count four by St. Michael's [Church] chimes, and I begin to hope. At half past four, the heavy booming of a cannon! I sprang out of bed and on my knees, prostrate [lying flat], I prayed as I never prayed before."

Every reader knows the story from here. The shelling of Fort Sumter started the great War Between the States, a war that cost six hundred thousand lives and untold suffering. Mary Boykin

---

People and Terms to Know

General Beauregard (BOH•ree•GAHRD)—P. G. T. Beauregard (1818–1893), Confederate general who ordered his troops to fire on Fort Sumter. He also participated in later battles in Tennessee, South Carolina, and Georgia.

Anderson—Major Robert Anderson (1805–1871), the Union commander of Fort Sumter when it was fired on by the Confederates.

Chesnut, although a born rebel, fully understood at the time the bold step the **Confederacy** was taking.

Many years have passed since Mary died in 1886. As I sit here, I think of all that she saw and heard. And I have come to this conclusion: I believe her wonderful diary will remain forever the best source of information available on how people in the South viewed the Civil War.

QUESTIONS TO CONSIDER

1. What about Mary Boykin Chesnut's life could make her book about the South during the Civil War interesting?

2. What did Mary mean when she said she was "of necessity a 'rebel born'"?

3. How did Mary feel on the day South Carolina seceded from the Union?

People and Terms to Know

Confederacy (kuhn•FEHD•uhr•uh•see)—Southern states that seceded from the United States in 1860 and 1861.

Sources

The Man and Machine That Changed History
by Judith Lloyd Yero

All the characters in this story are historical figures. The quotation about slavery comes from Solomon Northup's *Twelve Years a Slave: The Narrative of Solomon Northup*, David Wilson, ed. (Whitehall, NY, 1853). A good source of information on Eli Whitney and his inventions is *Eli Whitney and the Birth of American Technology* by Constance McLaughlin Green (Reading, MA: Addison Wesley Longman, Inc. 1999).

Fanny Kemble: Critic of Slavery *by Stephen Currie*

Both Nellie and Anna, the friend to whom Nellie writes her letter, are fictitious. Fanny Kemble and her husband, Pierce Butler, are historical. The source for the information in Nellie's letter comes from Fanny Kemble's *Journal of a Residence on a Georgia Plantation in 1838–1839* (University of Georgia Press, 1984).

Frederick Douglass's Escape to Freedom
by Lynnette Brent

Frederick Douglass is a historical figure, and the people and events described in this story are historically accurate. The source for information about Douglass's life is his own autobiography, *Narrative of the Life of Frederick Douglass, An American Slave, Written by Himself*, which was first published in 1845 by the Anti-Slavery Office in Boston.

P. T. Barnum and New York City *by Marianne McComb*

The characters in this story are all historical figures, and the events are historically accurate. The source is *P.T. Barnum: America's Greatest Showman* by Philip B. Kunhardt, Jr. (New York:. Knopf, 1995). Another interesting source for Barnum's life and career is his autobiography, *The Life of P. T. Barnum, Written by Himself* (University of Illinois Press, 2000), first published in 1855.

Put Up Your Dukes! *by Walter Hazen*
The boy who narrates this story is a fictional character, as are his parents. Henry Clay and the un-named editor of a Georgia newspaper are real, and the events described are historically accurate. A source for the comments the North and the South made about each other is *The Union Sundered* by T. Harry Williams (New York: Time Incorporated, 1963).

The Rebellion That Never Was *by Stephen Feinstein*
Jack is a fictional character. Denmark Vesey is a historical figure, and the information about him and his rebellion is historically accurate. Story sources include *Denmark Vesey* by David Robertson (New York: Alfred A. Knopf, 1999), and *Slaves in the Family* by Edward Ball (New York: Ballantine Books, 1998, 1999).

Angelina Grimké Starts a Riot *by Carole Pope*
The narrator is fictional. The people and events in the story are all real. For more information on Angelina Grimké, read *The Grimké Sisters from South Carolina: Pioneers for Women's Rights and Abolition* by Gerda Lerner (New York: Oxford University Press, 1998).

Harriet Tubman, "Railroad" Conductor *by Walter Hazen*
The narrator in this story is fictional. Harriet Tubman is a historical figure, and the information about her and her activities on the Underground Railroad are historically accurate. Sources for this story include *Days of Slavery: A History of Black People in America* by Stuart Kallen (Edina, MN.: Abdo & Daughters, 1990) and *A Pictorial History of African-Americans* by Langston Hughes and others (New York: Crown Publishers, Inc., 1995).

The Book That Helped to Start a War *by Judith Lloyd Yero*

The information about the effect of *Uncle Tom's Cabin* on feelings in the North is historically accurate. The story itself, told in digest form, is Stowe's own fiction. The full work is available in a reprint published in 1969 by Charles E. Merrill Publishing, Columbus, Ohio. Comments and quotations made by people of the times about the book and a further description of how the book influenced the country can be found in *Uncle Tom's Cabin and American Culture*, by Thomas F. Gossett (Dallas, TX: Southern Methodist University Press, 1985).

The Taking of Anthony Burns *by Stephen Currie*

The prison guard who narrates this story is fictional. Anthony Burns is a historical figure, and the events relating to his story are historically accurate. The source is *The Trials of Anthony Burns: Freedom and Slavery in Emerson's Boston* by Albert J. Von Frank, (Cambridge, MA: Harvard University Press, 1998).

Gold, Slavery, and Henry Clay *by Judith Lloyd Yero*

The information in this story is historically accurate. Sources include "How California Came to Be Admitted" by Rockwell D. Hunt, Ph.D., from the *San Francisco Chronicle*, September 9, 1900, "Clay's Resolutions of January 29, 1850" from the *U.S. Senate Journal, 31st Congress, 1st Session*, page 118, and the *Californian* of March 15 and May 20, 1848.

John Brown: Martyr or Murderer? *by Marianne McComb*

This story is historically accurate. John Brown is a historical figure. The source is *To Purge This Land with Blood: A Biography of John Brown* by Stephen B. Oates (New York: Harper and Row, 1970).

Blood on the Senate Floor *by Dee Masters*

The characters in this story are all historical figures, and the events are historically accurate. The source is *Charles Sumner and the Coming of the Civil War* (New York: Knopf, 1960), a Pulitzer Prize-winning biography by David Donald.

Dred Scott and the Supreme Court's Terrible Decision *by Judy Volem*

Sarah and Ruth are fictional characters. Dred Scott, his family members, his owners, and Chief Justice Roger Taney are historical figures. The events related are historically accurate. Sources include *Great American Trials,* Edward W. Knappman, editor (Detroit, MI: Visible Ink Press, a division of Gale Research Inc., 1994), *Black Mondays, Worst Decisions of the Supreme Court* by Joel D. Joseph (Bethesda, MD: National Press, 1987), and *The Oxford Companion to the Supreme Court of the United States,* Kermit L. Hall and others, editors (New York, Oxford: Oxford University Press, 1992).

Mary Boykin Chesnut: A Born Rebel *by Walter Hazen*

Mary Boykin Chesnut really lived, and the people she wrote about in her book are all historical figures. The events described are historically accurate. The source for the information in this story is *Mary Chesnut's Civil War* (New Haven, CT: Yale University Press, 1981), edited by C. Vann Woodward, which won the 1982 Pulitzer Prize in history.

Glossary of People and Terms to Know

abolition (AB•uh•LIHSH•uhn)—
act of ending slavery. A person who
wants to end slavery is called an
abolitionist.

Anderson, Robert—(1805–1871)
Union major who commanded Fort
Sumter when it was fired on by
the Confederates.

Anthony, Susan B.—(1820–1906)
one of the first campaigners for
women's rights, including the right
to vote.

arsenal (AHR•suh•nuhl)—place
for storing or repairing weapons
and ammunition.

Barnum, P. T.—(1810–1891)
Phineas Taylor Barnum, a multimillionaire American showman who
specialized in unusual, inexpensive
entertainment.

Bear Flag Republic—nation
proclaimed by American settlers
in California when they declared
independence from Mexico
in 1846.

Beauregard (BOH•ree•GAHRD)
P. G. T.—(1818–1893) Confederate
general who ordered his troops
to fire on Fort Sumter. He also
participated in later battles
in Tennessee, South Carolina,
and Georgia.

Brooks, Preston S.—(1819–1857)
U.S. representative from South
Carolina (1852–1857) who
attacked Senator Charles Sumner
in the Senate after Sumner's
verbal attack on his uncle Senator
Andrew P. Butler.

Brown, John—(1800–1859)
violent abolitionist who killed five
proslavery men in Kansas. In 1859,
he captured the U.S. arsenal at
Harpers Ferry (now in West
Virginia) as part of an effort to free
slaves. He was hanged in 1859.

Burns, Anthony—(c. 1834–1862)
young man who escaped from
slavery in Virginia and went to
Boston. In 1854 he was captured
by government agents and tried as
a runaway slave.

Butler, Pierce—(1806–1867)
member of an old Southern family,
owner of several hundred slaves on
a Sea Island plantation, and husband
of English actress Fanny Kemble.

Calhoun, John C.—(1782–1850)
statesman from South Carolina
who pushed the idea of states'
rights. He is best known for the
nullification theory, which held that,
under the Constitution, a state
had the right to cancel a federal
law that was harmful to it.

capitalists (KAP•ih•tihl•ihsts)—
people who lay out money (capital)
for something expected to make
a profit.

Chesnut, Mary Boykin—
(1823–1886) South Carolinian
whose diary provides a picture
of life in the South during the
Civil War.

Clay, Henry—(1777–1852) statesman who served as a U.S. senator
and a congressman from Kentucky.
Clay put together the Compromise
of 1850, which kept the Union
together for 10 more years.

cockades—knots of ribbon worn on hats as part of a military uniform.

compromise (KAHM•pruh•MYZ)—agreement in which each side in a dispute gives up some of its demands.

Compromise of 1850—series of laws meant to settle the disagreements between free states and slave states.

Confederacy (kuhn•FEHD•uhr•uh•see)— Southern states that seceded from the United States in 1860 and 1861.

cotton gin—machine that removes the seeds from the seed pod of the cotton plant. "Gin" comes from the word *engine*.

Davis, Jefferson—(1808–1889) only president of the Confederate States of America. He was charged with treason after the Civil War and imprisoned for two years.

disguise—use of changed dress or appearance to hide one's true identity.

Douglas, Stephen A.— (1813–1861) famed public speaker who served both as representative and senator from Illinois. Lincoln debated Douglas when he ran for Douglas's Senate seat.

Douglass, Frederick— (c. 1817–1895) runaway slave who became a famous Northern abolitionist, publisher, and public speaker. He advised Lincoln on slavery and later became U.S. Minister to Haiti.

economy (ih•KAHN•uh•mee)— way in which a country or region makes money; its business affairs.

financial depression—serious reduction in business activity. During a depression, many people lose their jobs.

forge—furnace where metals are heated and shaped.

Fort Sumter—Union fort at Charleston, South Carolina. In 1861 South Carolina requested that the commander of the fort surrender. The commander agreed to do so when his supplies ran out. Aware that new supplies were on the way, South Carolina refused his offer. On April 12, 1861, South Carolinian troops fired on the fort, and the Civil War started.

Fugitive (FYOO•jih•tihv) **Slave Act**—(1850) federal law that said U.S. citizens could be fined and arrested for helping to hide or rescue a runaway (fugitive) slave.

gold rush—rapid movement of many people to a region where gold has been discovered.

Grimké (GRIHM•kee) **Angelina**— (1805–1879) American antislavery and women's rights leader; sister of Sarah Grimké (1792–1873).

hostages (HAHS•tihj•uhs)— people held as prisoners until some demands are agreed to.

Irish peasants—here, poor immigrants from Ireland. Because of English governmental policies, Irish farmers and their families, who did not own the land they farmed, suffered from great poverty in the 1800s. As a result, many moved to the United States.

Kansas–Nebraska Act—(1854) law that established the Kansas and Nebraska territories and opened them for settlement. Residents would vote to decide whether their future states would be free or slave. Eventually, Kansas became a breeding ground for the Civil War because the North and the South each tried to send the most settlers into the new territory.

Kemble, Fanny—(1809–1893) English actress who married an American and spent some time living on his family's plantation. She became known as a strong critic of slavery.

King Cotton—term that recognizes that cotton growing was so important to the United States that the laws of the land would support it, just as if it were a king.

Lear—Shakespeare's play *King Lear.*

Legree, Simon—character in Harriet Beecher Stowe's *Uncle Tom's Cabin.* He is so fiercely cruel that his name has come to mean "a brutal taskmaster."

libel (LY•buhl)—crime of making damaging or false statements about a person.

Lind, Jenny—(1820–1887) talented singer born in Stockholm, Sweden. She toured the United States from 1850 to 1852.

marshals—law enforcement officials.

massacre (MAS•uh•kuhr)—killing of a group of people in an especially cruel way.

Mexican War—(1846–1848) war between Mexico and the United States. The war began after Mexico refused to accept U.S. annexation of Texas in 1845. After winning the war, the United States acquired Mexican territory from the Rio Grande to the Pacific coast.

millrace—stream of water that drives a mill wheel. Also called a raceway.

Missouri Compromise—(1820) law providing for the admission of Maine as a free state and Missouri as a slave state.

Moor's wife—leading role of Desdemona in William Shakespeare's play *Othello.* The Moor is a black North African named Othello, who is married to Desdemona and is the tragic hero of the play.

Moses—Hebrew prophet and lawgiver in the Bible who led the Israelites out of slavery in Egypt. Harriet Tubman was known as "Moses" for her role in leading slaves to freedom.

nullify (NUHL•uh•fy)—make it have no legal force.

overseers—people who keep watch over and direct the work of others, especially laborers.

patent (PAT•uhnt)—government grant that gives an inventor the sole right to make, use, and sell an invention for a set period of time.

Pierce, Franklin—(1804–1869) U.S. statesman, representative, and senator from New Hampshire who became the 14th president of the United States. He served as president from 1853 to 1857.

plantation (plan•TAY•shuhn)— large estate or farm on which crops are raised and harvested, often by people who live on the plantation.

Prince of Humbugs—nickname for P. T. Barnum. A humbug is something meant to fool people; a fake or hoax. Barnum loved to play pranks on people. Many of his exhibits turned out to be hoaxes, or fakes, but the crowds still loved his shows.

prospectors—people who explore an area for mineral deposits like gold or oil.

Quaker—member of a Christian group that opposes war and violence; also called the Society of Friends.

revolt—armed uprising; rebellion against a government.

Scott, Dred—(c. 1795–1858) American slave born in Virginia. He sued for his freedom after living for four years with his master in states where slavery had been banned by the Missouri Compromise. After a long court fight, the U.S. Supreme Court ruled in 1857 that he was not a citizen and was still a slave. The Missouri Compromise was declared unconstitutional.

Scottish play—William Shakespeare's *Macbeth,* which is set in Scotland. Many actors believe that it is bad luck to say the name of the play.

Sea Islands—group of islands in the Atlantic Ocean separated from the southeast coast of the United States by narrow channels.

secession (sih•SEHSH•uhn)—act of withdrawing from the Union (the United States).

spiritual—religious folksong originally created and sung by black slaves.

Stanton, Elizabeth Cady— (1815–1902) leader who worked throughout her life, much of the time in partnership with Susan B. Anthony, to help gain rights for women.

Stowe (stoh), **Harriet Beecher**—(1811–1896) author of *Uncle Tom's Cabin,* a book that greatly advanced the cause of abolition.

suffragists (SUHF•ruh•jists)— people who fight for the extension of voting rights, especially for women.

Sumner, Charles—(1811–1874) Republican senator from Massachusetts for four terms. He opposed slavery and the Fugitive Slave Act of 1850 and favored the right of blacks to vote. He was attacked in the Senate by a Southern congressman.

Taney (TAW•nee), **Roger B.**— (1777–1864) chief justice of the U.S. Supreme Court from 1836 to 1864. He wrote the majoritiy opinion in the *Dred Scott* case.

tariffs (TAIR•ihfs)—taxes on goods coming into or going out of a country.

The Tempest—play by Shakespeare set on a tropical island.

territory—part of the United States that is not a state but that has a governor and a legislature.

Toussaint (too•SAN) **L'Overture** (loo•veh•TOOR)—(c. 1743–1803) Haitian general and freedom fighter who helped Haiti win independence.

treason—high crime of betrayal of or disloyalty to one's country.

Tubman, Harriet—(c. 1820–1913) most famous "conductor" on the Underground Railroad. She led more than 300 slaves to freedom. Although she never learned to read or write, she became an effective antislavery speaker.

Uncle Tom—character in Harriet Beecher Stowe's *Uncle Tom's Cabin*. A hero in the novel, Uncle Tom has come to be an insulting term for a black person who gives in to a white person.

Underground Railroad—secret network by which runaway slaves were led to freedom in the North.

U.S. Supreme Court—highest court in the United States. Nine judges are nominated by the president with the "advice and consent" of the Senate. The judges serve for life. The role of the court is to see that the people's rights, according to the Constitution, are protected.

Vesey (VEE•zee), **Denmark**—(c. 1767–1822) free black carpenter who planned and organized a slave rebellion in South Carolina.

Whitney, Eli—(1765–1825) American inventor best known for his invention of the cotton gin. This invention changed the economy of the South. Whitney also invented the first machines that produced interchangeable parts.

Acknowledgements

10 © The Granger Collection.
11 © Culver Pictures.
13 © Scala/Art Resource, NY.
21 © North Wind Picture Archives.
24 Courtesy Library of Congress.
29 © Culver Pictures.
31 © Stock Montage, Inc.
35 © Culver Pictures.
37 © Bettman/Corbis.
40, 46, 48, 57 Courtesy Library of Congress.
59 © The Granger Collection.
65 © Bettman/Corbis.

70 © Culver Pictures.
73 © The Granger Collection.
79 Courtesy Library of Congress.
87 © Corbis.
95, 98, 101 Courtesy Library of Congress.
103, 110 © Corbis.
112, 119, 123, 130 © North Wind Picture Archives.
132, 140 © Corbis.
143 © The Granger Collection.
152, 159 © Corbis.
161 © The Granger Collection.